ACT WELL YOUR PART

» *There All the Honor Lies*

ACT WELL YOUR PART

» There All the
Honor Lies

A MEMOIR

Judge Harriet M. Murphy

FOREWORD BY PHYLICIA ALLEN RASHAD
PREFACE BY WILLIAM POWERS JR.

The Division of Diversity and Community Engagement »
The University of Texas at Austin » Distributed by Tower Books,
an Imprint of the University of Texas Press

© 2018 by Harriet Mitchell Murphy
Foreword © 2018 Phylicia Allen Rashad
Preface © 2018 William Powers Jr.
All rights reserved.
Printed in the United States of America.
First edition, 2018
Distributed by Tower Books, an Imprint of the University of Texas Press
All photos are from the author's personal collection, unless otherwise noted.

Requests for permission to reproduce material from this work should be sent to:
Permissions
University of Texas Press
P.O. Box 7819
Austin, TX 78713-7819
http://utpress.utexas.edu/index.php/rp-form

♾ The paper used in this book meets the minimum requirements of ANSI/NISO Z39.48-1992 (R1997) (Permanence of Paper).

LIBRARY OF CONGRESS CATALOGING-IN-PUBLICATION DATA
Names: Murphy, Harriet M., (Judge), author.
Title: There all the honor lies : a memoir / judge Harriet M. Murphy.
Description: First edition. | Austin : Tower Books, an imprint of the University of Texas Press, 2018. | Includes bibliographical references.
Identifiers: LCCN 2018008994
    ISBN 978-1-4773-1574-3 (cloth : alk. paper)
    ISBN 978-1-4773-1575-0 (library e-book)
    ISBN 978-1-4773-1630-6 (non-library e-book)
Subjects: LCSH: Murphy, Harriet M., (Judge) | Women judges—Texas—Biography. | African American judges—Texas—Biography.
Classification: LCC KF373.M84 M84 2018 | DDC 347.764/0234 [B]—dc23
LC record available at https://lccn.loc.gov/2018008994

DOI: 10.7560/315743

for
The University of Texas
Division of Diversity and Community Engagement
and especially
Vice President Dr. Gregory J. Vincent

»

Honor and shame from no condition rise;
Act well your part, there all the honor lies.
—ALEXANDER POPE

Friends say, "Harriet, where you get all that energy from?"
I say, "I don't think I have any left now!"

Contents

Foreword » Phylicia Rashad xi
Preface » William Powers Jr. xiii
Acknowledgments xv
Timeline: The Black Migration xvii

PART I » STONY THE ROAD 1

Real and Necessary and Powerful Change 3
Fulton County, Georgia 4
Grade School 7
Celebrating the Good Times 10
A Fruitful Faith 11
High School 13
Atlanta's Caste System 16
F Is for *Fun* 18
Spending Money 20
Playing Hooky 22
Meeting W. E. B. Du Bois 24
Other Formative Experiences from a Georgia Childhood 26
The Spelman Years 28
History and Government 31
The Black Renaissance 33
Mitchell versus UGA 36
Thurgood to the Rescue 38
Johns Hopkins University (JHU) Fellowship 40
The Year of Benjamin Brown 43

PART II » EARLY CAREER 47

An Evening with MLK Jr. 49

Mitchell, Meet Moore 51

The Civil Rights Act of 1964 and More NAACP 53

O. J.'s Death 55

Law School at UT 57

Mitchell, Meet Murphy 61

One Last Bid for Change 65

A Kerfuffle over the Bar Exam 66

Huston-Tillotson Gets a Pre-Law Society 68

Examining Apartheid in South Africa 69

On Blood Diamonds 72

Foreign Reaction to the Montgomery Bus Boycott 73

Travel to Gratz, Austria 75

Harriet Murphy, JD 77

Why Black Lawyers Had It Harder 79

PART III » MAJOR POLITICAL CONTRIBUTIONS 81

Carter for the Win 83

Murphy's Law 86

Accomplishments from the Bench 90

Here Come the Judges 92

"Retirement" 95

Vacation Time! 97

The O. J. Simpson Trial 99

Abigail Fisher and the Top 10 Percent Rule 102

Judge Murphy Goes on *Judge Judy* 105

PART IV » THERE ALL THE HONOR LIES 109

Afterword   131

*Appendix I » Reverend Walter M. Mitchell Sr.:
Minister and Civil Rights Activist*   133

Appendix II » List of Awards   139

References   143

Foreword

I have known Judge Murphy for many years. When I was in elementary school, my father married Eleanor Hall, one of Harriet's best friends, and so it was that she was a frequent guest in our home and also at social gatherings. We lived in Houston, Texas. Harriet was a professor at Prairie View A&M College (now Prairie View A&M University). She was brilliant, jovial, unassuming, kind, and always accessible.

Events both fortuitous and unfortunate kept bringing us together. When there was a death in the family—my father's, Eleanor's, Eleanor's sister—Harriet was there to offer consolation. In 2005, I was awarded the Texas Medal of Arts, and Harriet opened her home in Austin to host me. When my sister, Debbie Allen Nixon, and I received honorary doctorates from Spelman College in 2011, Harriet showed up to celebrate with us. Through it all, we have kept up with each other's achievements and renewed our friendship. I am honored to know her and very proud of who she is and all that she has accomplished in service to our people and our community. That is why I wanted to assist in framing the story you are about to read.

So, I'll start with a question first posed by staff writer Marilyn Marshall in an *Austin American-Statesman* article dated October 5, 1975: "The montage of historically famous blacks above [Murphy's] desk, does not include her but who's to say that someday it will not?" Marshall goes on to detail the then-to-date lifetime achievements of Harriet Mitchell Murphy as a "judge, lawyer, professor, community leader, and a woman with a great sense of black pride." Judge Murphy had just received another "honor for Her Honor," this time bestowed by the Association of Colleges and Universities for International Intercultural Studies (ACUIIS) in Washington, DC. The award recognized Judge Murphy's leadership role in several faculty and student

projects that promoted intercultural dialogue—adding to an already-long list of prestigious accolades and earned degrees.

While this book is, in keeping with Judge Murphy's wishes, a "most thorough" account of her life and times—in particular of what she and other African American activists have referred to as The Struggle for civil rights—*Act Well Your Part* highlights only her most outstanding awards. A complete list, spanning over five decades, may be found on the pages that immediately follow. As you read, learn from, and enjoy this book, I think you will agree that Harriet Murphy is a remarkable and truly inspiring woman who has joined the montage of historically famous African Americans, assuming her rightful place for all time.

Phylicia Rashad
2016

PHYLICIA ALLEN RASHAD is an actress and stage director best known for her role as Claire Huxtable on *The Cosby Show*. In 2004, she became the first black actress to win a Tony Award for best actress in a play. Phylicia is also the stepdaughter of Eleanor Allen, one of Harriet Murphy's oldest and dearest friends.

Preface

I should make a confession at the start: Judge Harriet Murphy is a good friend. So I can't really be objective—but that doesn't mean that what I say about her and her memoirs isn't true.

When I became dean of the UT law school in 2000, we were suffering from the aftermath of the Hopwood case, in which it was ruled that we could not take race or ethnicity into account in our admissions standards. We were down to five African American students in our entering class. Many people helped turn that around but none more so than Harriet Murphy. She helped connect me and the law school to the African American community in Austin and beyond. From the State Bar of Texas to the National Bar Association, her efforts to involve African American lawyers throughout the United States made a *big* difference.

My subsequent appointment in 2006 as president of the university gave Murphy a larger stage on which to mount our campaign. She had, of course, been a very active supporter of my predecessor, Larry Faulkner, in his efforts to diversify the campus, but she seemed to redouble her efforts when I moved to the Tower. I recall a time when she waited all day at a legislative hearing to testify on a bill that was important to UT.

So far, this is the story of a good friend—yes, a good friend of mine, a good friend of the law school, and a good friend of the university. But something even more important makes this memoir so powerful, and so touching. When Harriet Murphy enrolled at Spelman in 1945, she was barred *by law* from enrolling in the very place that would become her beloved University of Texas; she was barred from its law school as well. For today's readers, especially today's young readers, that is the story in the pages of this book that should not be forgotten. It is the story of a young African American woman who came of age when the civil rights battle was only beginning, in a time when Jim Crow was *legal*, when Rosa Parks was riding the bus in Montgomery, Alabama, and when cases like *Brown v. Board of Education* and *Sweatt v. Painter* determined the fate of desegregation at institutions like the University of Texas School of Law.

Harriet Murphy finally entered the UT law school in the 1960s, along with a group of pioneers who came to be known as the Precursors: dedicated alumni who stayed together and worked to make the university more inclusive. Harriet Murphy was their glue. She achieved much in her professional career, stacking up award after award, and eventually assumed her place in the judiciary. But her most notable achievement may well have been her impact on UT.

In December 2007, UT (with the help of Judge Murphy) held its first annual Community Leadership Awards Ceremony in East Austin. The ceremony has since come to be a wonderful yearly holiday party, at which we always honor Harriet Murphy. I recall at that first party having a conversation with an African American alumna. She thanked me for having the event, and then she said, "All I ever wanted to do was love my alma mater." This was from a woman who years before had been discriminated against. That, I thought, was a testament to the human spirit, which Harriet Murphy embodies in her life also. That is what this memoir is all about.

William Powers Jr.
2016

WILLIAM POWERS JR. was the twenty-eighth president of the University of Texas (UT) at Austin (2006–2015). Prior to that appointment, he served as the dean of UT's School of Law. Powers was president when Abigail Fisher's lawsuit (2008) was brought against the university, prompting national scrutiny of the state's Top 10 Percent Rule (detailed in part III of this book).

Acknowledgments

A tremendous and heartfelt thank-you to every single person mentioned in or who otherwise influenced this book. Look at everything we created together!

To Dr. Herschell Shelley: a sincere thank-you for your research contributions. A thank you, also, to Jessica Hagemann at Cider Spoon Stories for her help in preparing the manuscript.

To M. L. and all those activists of my generation who, in holding our self-image to be important, stood on the backs of Atlanta's black leaders: we should be proud of, and not surprised by, all we have accomplished. To the next generation: there is still much work to be done, but I know we can count on you.

Pat, I miss and love you every day.

Timeline: The Black Migration

1860s: My great-grandmother Harriet Willis lives in slavery until she is six. With the issuing of Lincoln's Emancipation Proclamation, she and her mother are freed. Harriet grows up to bear thirteen freeborn children. Many years later, we listen to such stories as Harriet can remember, but as a child, I lack the frame of reference to grasp their real significance.

1900s: My grandfather, a minister from Madison, Georgia, marries my mother's mother. When my grandmother dies, he takes their four children, including my mother, Florida Mitchell, to live with great-grandmother Harriet in Atlanta. Harriet is in poor health, and the children go largely unsupervised. None of them receive more than an eighth-grade education before they start working.

1920s: My mother names me after my great-grandmother Harriet—who was herself named for Harriet Tubman. I meet my biological father, Alfonso Simpson, of Washington, Georgia. The descendant of a female slave and her white master, Alfonso is a budding artist and works as a janitor. I keep one of his early paintings in the entryway of my home.

Early 1930s: My grandfather asks me to call him Daddy rather than Granddaddy, because he's courting again after my grandmother's death and doesn't want to seem old. He gives me an allowance, and I love him dearly, so I acquiesce. "Daddy" marries a beautiful young woman who gives him two more children. He divorces her before becoming involved with the civil rights movement in Madison. My grandfather—the reverend—gets run out of Madison because of his outspoken activism. Having both some formal and ministerial education, he is very smart and aligns himself early on with the Democratic Party.

Late 1930s: My mother marries my stepfather, Walter McClarity. Although I know Mom loves Walter a lot, I want nothing to do with him, so I keep my last name. My father has moved to Kansas City to open a general store and attend art school. I start taking the train to visit him in the summers. Grandpa marries wife number three, a schoolteacher named Hazeltine, and they have my aunt Rosalyn. Rosalyn becomes the first black woman to get a PhD at Emory. She teaches at Spelman and Morehouse Colleges and eventually goes to work for the federal government.

Early 1940s: These are the years I start visiting my father in Kansas City. During World War II, social workers are stationed inside the train hubs. One day on my way to visit Dad, a good-looking soldier approaches me at St. Louis. He flirts and offers to take me shopping. I pick up my bags to leave with him, but a social worker intervenes. She tells me to keep my butt in the station, that she'll be watching me. That's good, because I don't have any better sense.

Mid-1940s: Dad gets remarried and has another daughter, my half sister, Berniece. She has the same green eyes as I do, and the salesmen always say, "Look, here come those two green-eyed women!" Berniece and I are close until the 1980s, when Dad puts $80,000 of his money in her name and it soon disappears. He begs me to find it. Since Dad has hurt my feelings by not allowing me to be a part of the transfer of the funds, I should stay out of the situation. Instead, I get a lawyer and take her to court, and it ruins my relationship with Berniece.

Late 1940s: I start school at Spelman College. Dad pays for my dorm room, and Mom brings me pork chop sandwiches. This period of my life is the closest I have ever been to her.

1950s: A black realtor encourages the one hundred or so blacks living in Johnsontown (including my mother and Walter) to sell out. The land becomes very desirable; a shopping center replaces our neighborhood. A black exodus occurs to Chicago, New York, and California. My mother and stepfather consider Chicago but decide to stay in Georgia after Walter visits the Windy City and finds more roaches and rats than opportunities. I earn a master's in political science from Atlanta University and move to Baton Rouge, Louisiana, to teach at Southern University. Two years later, I start teaching at Prairie View University.

1950s: I marry Dr. O. J. Moore, in Longview, Texas. O. J. works at a small hospital clinic. We have no children. I begin to teach at the black high school.

1960s: I stay in touch with Berniece's kids and grandkids and treat them like my own. My husband, Pat (who I meet while in law school at the University of Texas at Austin [UT]), and I attend all their graduations and weddings. One of Berniece's sons, Mark Berry, is an emergency doctor in Birmingham; he still comes to visit me. Another, Glen Berry, is a physician at Prairie View A&M University.

1970s: I remember the importance of family and reach out to Rosalyn and her son. Rosalyn reminds me of my grandfather, the person from my family whom I was closest to and who made the greatest impact on my life. Meanwhile, I'm teaching government at Huston-Tillotson (H-T) University and practicing law part-time.

1980s–2000s: I take a judgeship and complete most of the community advocacy work that earns me the awards listed on the previous pages.

2013: Pat and I play competitive bridge until his death.

2015: I decide to write a book. This is my legacy.

ACT WELL YOUR PART

» *There All the Honor Lies*

PART I » STONY THE ROAD

Stony the road we trod,
Bitter the chastening rod,
Felt in the days when hope unborn had died;
Yet with a steady beat,
Have not our weary feet
Come to the place for which our fathers sighed?
—JAMES WELDON JOHNSON

» *Real and Necessary and Powerful Change*

This is a book about aspiration and achievement—about deciding I wanted to do a thing and then doing it. My race, of course, was the big stop sign standing in my way. I was born in 1929 into the heart of southern American genteelism; slavery was long over, but state-mandated segregation was just rearing its ugly head. I spent the better part of my life fighting in solidarity with, and for, my black brothers and sisters against a system that, when it came down to it, was nothing more than white men's words on paper. Lucky for all of us, laws are overturned as easily as they are made. The triad of checks and balances in the United States leaves plenty of room for judicial advocacy, for the voices of common people and the officials they elect to effect real change when it is needed. That's why I became a lawyer and, ultimately, a judge at a time when black women, in particular, were not expected, encouraged, or sometimes even allowed to do so. I was blessed with a brain and a dauntless will, and I've used them fearlessly all my life.

That's not to say I was never humbled by, never downright terrified of, a world that seemed intent on knocking me back. We called it The Struggle because while there may have been no literal shackles, black America was grappling with restraints and constraints all the same. Most of us tried to shuck our chains civilly, working peaceably within the society that bound us. When James Earl Ray shot and killed the Reverend Martin Luther King Jr. in 1968, however, it touched off a violent reaction that continues today with the increasing number of black victims of police brutality. That so few of the offending officers sworn to uphold the law and protect the citizenry are themselves ever convicted suggests we're still not getting it right in this country.

And yet, I have seen change—real and necessary and powerful change—just in my lifetime. So, let's go back to where my story starts.

» *Fulton County, Georgia*

Although unusual by today's standards, the story of my birth was fairly commonplace back then. I was delivered at home by a midwife who failed to report my birth to the county, so for many years I didn't exist as far as Georgia was concerned. I never knew about the discrepancy until I tried to go to high school and the administrators asked for a copy of my birth certificate. My mother confessed she didn't have one, so being the enterprising upstart that I was, I marched my fourteen-year-old self down to the State Office of Vital Records, acquired the proper forms, filled them out (not bothering to consult my mother), and had my notary-public cousin authorize them. Because I had no idea how old I really was, I picked the age I wanted to be: sixteen, the age of the "popular" girls I was running around with in those days. Thus, while the 1940 census rightfully records my birth year as 1929, for my whole life I've used 1927 instead.

It's funny, I suppose, as well as a little sad, that as a child I didn't know my own age. But that was the situation. My mom was a single mother who was sometimes more interested in dating men than in raising me. We lived in an uptown section of Atlanta called Buckhead, which was and still is the most affluent area of the city. As in Clarksville here in Austin, there were pockets of the black community nestled within the majority-white district, and Mother and I kept our modest home on Dunwoody Road in one such pocket. Of course, the white neighborhoods had paved roads, whereas most of the black neighborhoods had dirt roads. We were lucky to live at the intersection between the two; we had a paved road! In those days, our particular pocket was called Willistown, after my great-grandmother. She'd been one of the first to settle in the area, which had originally been a wilderness, just as soon as she was freed from slavery.

My father, meanwhile, lived in Kansas City. We had an okay rela-

My mother, Florida Mitchell McClarity

tionship despite the distance. Once I got old enough to travel alone, at maybe ten or twelve years old, I started taking the train to spend summers with him in Kansas. We stayed relatively close even later in life; I was closer to him anyway than I was to my mother.

I suppose I passed the time the way that most poor kids did back then: by making my own fun. We used to build "houses" out of fallen pine boughs, complete with leafy beds and other furniture. In late summer, when the blackberries ripened, we picked and mashed the berries to make "wine." It was an arduous process that involved leaving the berries to ferment in glass jars and then boiling and straining them. Our wine was more rancid juice than alcohol, but we drank it proudly and called it good.

Around the time I turned six, Mother and I moved from Dunwoody Road to Bagley Park, another black section of Buckhead. One night when I was seven or eight years old, the Ku Klux Klan came stomping down our road. Our unpaved road was off the main street, and there was a church on the corner. There must have been hundreds of those peaked white hoods, and there were torches in every other hand. Even someone who didn't know to be scared of the hate that the Klan represented might have turned tail and fled anyway, with that large group looking like so many angry ghosts. Not me. From where my family had been sitting on our porch, I ran straight up to the front of the marchers and warned them that our street dead-ended—they'd go walking right into the woods if they kept on. (You can see that I nurtured a civic mind-set from an early age.) The KKK leader could have struck me or worse for my seeming impudence, but my terrified cousin had run right out after me and was pulling me back even as I was yelling my warning. They must have believed me, because they all turned around and walked right back out—leaving naught but a single burning cross on the church lawn.

» *Grade School*

Atlanta was special in that it had both a city school district and a county school district. I went to Fulton County School, which served all the little towns for miles around. Naturally, the school was all black, with four black teachers for grades one through seven. Because bus service existed only for the white schools, black students walked to school from wherever they called home. The walk was about a mile for me from our house on Dunwoody Road to the one-room Fulton County School building.

Starting when I was three years old, a teacher named Ms. Reynolds would stop and pick me up and take me to school with her while my mother went to work as a domestic servant. I was too young to be in school, and yet, I tell you, that experience had everything to do with the early development of my intelligence. All day long I sat and listened to the students, some as old as twelve, recite their lessons, so that by the time I was a student myself, I was much advanced for my age. Eventually I started tutoring those of my classmates who struggled to learn the material.

For most of my grade-school years, we lived in Bagley Park in Buckhead. The Park, as we called it, no longer exists on any Atlanta map, but it's still a term of endearment for those who are alive to remember it. I hold on to the memory of The Park because, in addition to being one of just two Fulton County students to graduate high school, I was the very first resident of Bagley Park to go to college—quite the distinction!

The same year that Mother and I moved to Bagley Park, the student body outgrew its one-room schoolhouse. The grade school relocated to a four-room building in Johnsontown, and Ms. Reynolds became its new principal. Johnsontown was an even farther walk from home, but walk we did. All that walking meant that up until the time

I graduated from high school, I never weighed more than one hundred pounds.

Under *Plessy v. Ferguson*, which dictated separate-but-equal services and facilities for blacks and whites, Fulton County had to subsidize the school. We received food-stamp-quality lunch provisions from the state, but there was no budget with which to hire a kitchen staff. Ms. Reynolds therefore recruited parent volunteers to make the lunches on a rotating basis in an empty building next to the school. The fruit the state supplied she turned around and sold to the students for five cents per apple or orange. I know this because fruit selling was my classroom chore. Certainly it was illegal, but with the extra money raised, Ms. Reynolds built a tennis court on the grounds. Although none of us could play tennis, her son was an outstanding tennis player, and he used the court as his personal practice platform.

That wasn't the only way Ms. Reynolds manipulated the power of her position to her own advantage. After the tennis court went in, she next crusaded for electric lights. The school didn't have any, which precluded using the building for PTA meetings or other activities at night. Ms. Reynolds's grand idea was to send the students door-to-door in the afternoons to rich, white folks' homes and beg for change. Those were the days when blacks went to the back door; we would not have been allowed to knock on a white person's front door. As it turned out, the white community was quite sympathetic to children with no lights, and together we raised a bundle.

Only later did I find out that Fulton County subsidized the installation of electric lights that year, and Ms. Reynolds likely pocketed all our profits. She was a well-educated, obviously crafty black woman. Her husband was an editor for Atlanta's black paper. Both were well known and respected, and nobody thought to question her—not about the lights and not when she convinced the churches in Buckhead to let us have Christmas and Easter programs for contributions.

Nevertheless, she really did care for her students. Once in a while, we all benefited from her wily ways. For example, she decreed that sixth and seventh graders during the spring semester could choose to do schoolwork or to work in the flower beds on the school's grounds. Those of us who chose to be outside won the district prize for most beautiful landscaping that year for our school. Plus, working in the flower beds meant we didn't have to go to class!

There was also the day Ms. Reynolds came to school with a maternity dress. Holding it high for all the girls to see, she said, "I have this beautiful dress here today, and I was wondering if a student might like to have it. Would anyone like to wear it?" Of course I held my hand up, along with most of the girls in the room. Finally, one girl raised her hand, and Ms. Reynolds said to her, "I think this dress would really fit you. I want you to wear it every day. You can wash it in the evenings, and iron it." None of us but Ms. Reynolds realized that the girl was pregnant. That's why she'd brought the dress, for her! It should be noted that that girl's classroom chore was to help the parents cook lunch, so the principal had good reason for wanting to keep her at school. Still, those were crazy days.

» *Celebrating the Good Times*

One thing Mama did very well was parties. Whether for my birthday or the holidays, she always went all out as much as she was able. At my birthday parties, she served homemade ice cream, having spent all that time hand churning the milk and the sugar inside a metal-lined, wooden container packed with ice and rock salt. Every time, I ate that ice cream to the point of illness.

On Christmas, no matter how strapped we were that year for money, Mama magically produced gifts, food, and fruit. At Easter, there were new shoes, a hat, and a dress. One Easter I remember begging for a pair of patent-leather shoes that were really too small for me. I cried until she bought them, and then I wore them even though they hurt my feet.

I'd be remiss here if I didn't mention Thanksgiving and New Year's. These two holidays and the black community go together like chitlins and pickled pig feet. Chitlins are the guts of a pig boiled with potatoes. Pig feet are exactly what they sound like. Sometimes I cook them in a pressure cooker. During slavery, whites wouldn't eat these foods, so they were given to the slaves. To this day, they're popular foods in the black community, but they are also why blacks have such a high rate of heart disease and high blood pressure. It's from eating all that pork! Almost all my great-uncles and great-aunts died of strokes or heart attacks due to poor diet.

» *A Fruitful Faith*

Religion has always been important to me. Starting when I was little, Margaret Guest (mother of the late, great William Guest, of Gladys Knight and the Pips fame!) would take me to Sunday services at Piney Grove Baptist Church in Buckhead. My own mother wasn't religious at the time (despite her father being a minister), so I guess Mrs. Guest took it upon herself to save my soul. Through her and the rest of the Guests (who *all* had wonderful singing voices), I was exposed to revival meetings, the Baptist Young People's Union (BYPU), Bible study, and more. It was at the home of another Piney Grove member that I first learned to recite the Lord's Prayer. At the age of eight, I joined the Piney Grove Baptist Church. By thirteen, I had become the clerk of the very small country church. My duties included keeping track of parishioners' donations and taking minutes at church business meetings.

Many years later, after commercial development and gentrification had forced most of the black community to move out of Buckhead, I tried to locate the Piney Grove church. The church had moved to Atlanta as an outgrowth of the church I had originally attended. Even though there was a cemetery on the grounds, I was unsuccessful in finding out what happened to the parishioners, both living and buried. It seems that everyone became members of other churches, and the church probably disbanded.

In Atlanta, I joined Bethel Baptist, a church that had broken away from the church of Martin Luther King Jr.'s father. In high school, Martin Luther was called M. L. instead of by his full name, and most of us who knew him called him M. L. all his life. Bethel Baptist was the very church in which M. L. would go on to preach his maiden sermon. I was in attendance for that sermon, and both the issues he addressed and his powerful delivery of them have never left me. With the exception of the two years I taught at Prairie View College (now Prairie View A&M University), I have always been a member of a church—and as I've gone from church to church and thus witnessed many different ministers, I've yet to meet one who impressed me as much as M. L. I get bored when I go to church and all the minister preaches about is the Bible. There are larger issues at hand. Churches should be leaders in improving the quality of black life in this country!

» *High School*

Thanks, I'm sure, to my premature start in education, I graduated valedictorian of my seventh-grade class. High school started with eighth grade, and I was placed on the academic track, meant for those students who were college bound. Booker T. Washington High School had three tracks: academic (which required Latin, a foreign language, history, and math), business (which consisted mostly of classes in dictation, typing, and bookkeeping for female would-be secretaries), and vocational (which was geared toward boys and manual labor). I recall one of the vocational teachers once asking for more equipment to "help his students be more successful"; the principal's reply was that "all we want are students who can change tires and wipe windshields." Apparently, the goal was not to produce first-class mechanics but passable service-station attendants.

Booker T. Washington High School was in the Washington Park neighborhood, even farther from Bagley Park than Johnsontown. I was reduced to taking the public bus to school until finally I moved in with Aunt Ida Britton in Atlanta. Between her husband and her work, my mother was too distracted to even notice my absence, and the Brittons's household provided a much more stable and supportive environment. Aunt Ida wasn't actually my blood aunt but the aunt of my grandfather's third wife. I got to know her because every time Grandpa and his wife came to visit Aunt Ida, I would go stay there too; eventually Ida asked whether I wouldn't just move in with her, both to help out around the house and to keep her company when her brick mason husband was away on a job. I lived at the Brittons's house even partway through college, which is probably another reason that my mother and I grew apart.

For being the only black public high school in Atlanta, Booker T.

was an excellent school that graduated many leaders. Martin Luther King Jr. went there; he was in fact my same age. (We were both born in 1929, but as I was going by 1927 as a birth year at that time, he was a grade or two below me.) Martin Luther King Jr. and I were on a first-name basis then. Early evidence of Dr. King's eventual oratory prowess can be found in the Booker T. Washington class of 1944 yearbook, which featured M. L.'s essay on "The Negro and the Constitution." The essay highlights the contradictions between America's biblical faith and constitutional values and condemns the continuing problem of racial discrimination: "My heart throbs anew in the hope that inspired by the example of Lincoln, imbued with the spirit of Christ, [America] will cast down the last barrier to perfect freedom," wrote King. "And I with my brother of blackest hue possessing at last my rightful heritage and holding my head erect, may stand beside the Saxon—a Negro—and yet a man!"

At only fifteen years old, M. L. was powerfully aware of the black situation. He wasn't reading about it in books; he was living it, surrounding himself with black mentors like the Reverend William Holmes Borders (a man well known for walking the walk and talking the talk, he led the campaign to desegregate Atlanta's public transportation in the 1950s). It was M. L.'s activism that made me question for the first time my own social standing and the cultural structures that were in fact shackles. On overhearing a white woman once dismiss MLK Jr. as an "opportunist," I sent her that passage from the yearbook to show her he didn't just come on the scene during the heyday of the civil rights movement but was pondering racial inequality at an age when most boys cared only for sports and girls.

For my part, I cared more for boys than anything else in high school. The sixteen-year-olds that I'd fallen in with were fast and trendy and quickly destroyed any lingering naïveté from my years in quiet Buckhead. I benefited greatly not only from Aunt Ida's relaxed authority but also from her husband's skin color. Mr. Britton was technically black, but he looked very white and even in his job could pass for a white person. This distinction was important because, in addition to the class system, Atlanta had a caste system—one that said the lighter skinned you were, the easier life itself would be.

It's part of why I fell for George. The extremely light-skinned son of a doctor, he'd been sent to Atlanta by a father who felt that the schools in Americus, Georgia, were not good enough for George. We used to stand in the halls and watch him walk to class, giggling and touching our hair.

» *Atlanta's Caste System*

I am light skinned for a black woman. I also possess a most unusual quality among blacks: bright-green eyes. It goes back to the plantation. My ancestors were slaves to a Dr. Simpson, a Scot with red hair and green eyes. It was common practice then for slave owners to bed their female slaves and for children to be born of the union. Many times, the mixed-race kids looked more white than black. Down through the ages, white-looking blacks tended to marry partners who looked like them, effectively creating their own color-based caste system.

It was from such a series of unions that my father ultimately descended. His grandfather, not having a surname of his own, had assumed the Simpson moniker (also a common plantation practice). Therefore, my father's name was Simpson too. Since he never married my mother, however, I stuck with her maiden name: Mitchell.

Likely it was my own higher place in this caste system that kept me ignorant of racism for so long—that and, although I wasn't aware of it until later, my own self-defeating acceptance of "the way things were." Before I moved in with the Brittons, I had to ride the bus to Booker T. from Bagley Park. Black people rode in the back of the bus, and as I was black, I did too. I never really thought a thing of it—certainly not that it was strange, or wrong, or unfair. Then one day, four or five Muslim women, dark skinned and with their hair covered, boarded the bus and sat near the front. Nobody said a word about it. That was the first time I thought maybe something was off. What real differences were there between them and me? Between me and a white woman, for that matter?

The other rule about public transportation was that blacks could enter a bus or streetcar using the front door but always had to exit by the back door. One afternoon I was out shopping with girlfriends,

My half sister, Berniece, and me with our father, Alfonso Simpson

and we were all riding at the back of a streetcar. I noticed a huge black man, looking like he'd come straight from a construction job, pay his fare, board the car, and take a seat in the back. When his stop came up, this man exited through the front door. Because of what happened next, I really don't think it was some act of protest or rebellion. The streetcar driver threw the vehicle into park, jumped off the car, and accosted the man. "*YOU* can't go out the front door!" he yelled. "*YOU* gotta go out the back!" And just like that, the huge black man let the white driver pull him back onto the car and push him back out the rear exit.

In a rare fit, I then stood and yelled at the black man through the door. "Look, sir! You don't have to go to no back. Why'd you let that man take you back on the car? Big as you are. Why'd you let him pull you back on the car?" You could have heard a pin drop after that outburst. A whole car full of blacks, and me, a girl! My girlfriends said later that they wouldn't go back to town with me, as my behavior was liable to get us all thrown in jail.

» *F Is for Fun*

As it was, those girls were the ones who later got me in trouble. From playing hooky to drooling over boys, we thought *f* was for *fun*, and we didn't worry about *flunking*.

The night of the school dance at the USO, I met up with a friend and her boyfriend. Who did they have with them but George—that light-skinned king of the high-school hallways! To my disbelief, George asked if I would accompany him. My mama gave her approval, but darn if I didn't have to fight George off in the back seat all the way to the dance and home again. The redeeming part was that all the girls at the dance saw me there with him, and it improved my reputation considerably. They figured if I had what it took to show up with George, I was good enough to run with the best of them. I was invited the very next day to join a popular clique of girls with whom I would become lifelong friends. Those girls and I double-dated a lot but I never did have a boyfriend in high school, as I felt that some of my friends had eyes for guys that I liked, and there was jealousy. The next time I saw George, he was married and had a family.

When my girlfriends and I weren't going to dances, we danced in physical-education class. The dance teacher was Haitian and also taught French at Booker T. Washington. One semester, we practiced endlessly for our big fund-raiser production, which was some epic story told entirely through dance. At practice on the day before the affair, I got out of step and messed up the sequence. Do you know that teacher walked right up to me and slapped me? Hard! My first instinct was to hit her back, but my friend and the star of the show, Mattiwilda Dobbs, intervened. "She's just nervous," Mattiwilda consoled me. "She wants the show to go off perfectly. You're gonna do fine." Indeed, my performance was on point the next night, and that teacher ended up leaving the school soon after. I never liked studying

French under an American teacher after that because the French accent just wasn't right. As for Mattiwilda, she went on to become an internationally acclaimed opera singer who was invited to the University of Texas two or three times as a visiting music professor.

Sadly, my one-time stage performance had convinced me I had some dancing talent, when in fact I had no such thing. A couple of Morehouse fraternity brothers later asked me and another woman to dance in their performance (who knows why), which only bloated my ego further. I remember going home to Aunt Ida and announcing: "I don't want to go to college; I want to go to New York and dance with Katherine Durham." She promptly pooh-poohed the notion, stating that society equated dancers with prostitutes. It was the late 1940s, so she may have been right. At any rate, I didn't go to New York that year.

» Spending Money

I have worked since I was fourteen years old. It began with babysitting. Buckhead was so wealthy that plenty of families could afford to pay for hired help; among them were the Dickeys. The Dickeys kept a maid who lived in Bagley Park, and it was their maid who recommended me to them. They were a young couple with a beautiful baby. They lived with the elder Mr. and Mrs. Dickey in a very fine house. Sometimes I wandered around that house while the baby was asleep, and one time I noticed a silver service set that had been gifted to Mr. Dickey by President Roosevelt. The older Mr. and Mrs. Dickey traveled a lot, which is why they couldn't always help care for the baby. I babysat an average of once a week, walking all the way there after school and accepting a ride home from the baby's father at night.

Later, I took a part-time job at a restaurant. My friend Miss Pauline was the head cook there, so she got the restaurant's manager to hire me. After school and on some weekends, I waitressed, helped with food prep, and washed dishes as needed. The owner of the restaurant was very nice and always gave Miss Pauline and me a ride home. The owner's sister, though, was very prejudiced. She used to treat Miss Pauline so badly that Miss Pauline once pulled a stunt just like Minny did in *The Help*. It wasn't a "shit pie" that Miss Pauline served, but she did take the whole chicken that she was about to roast for the owner's sister and put it in the toilet bowl before cooking it. She flushed the lever a couple of times to get it good and washed in toilet water before popping it into the oven. Miss Pauline's reaction was typical of how blacks felt about racist people. I never had problems like that with the Dickeys, who were a very prominent family and knew how to treat everyone well.

During summer breaks, I worked at Davison's department store (the precursor to Macy's). This job was fabulous for a couple of reasons. First, every time the store had an outlet sale, all the employees got first dibs. We combed over the sale racks in the basement of clothes not sold, and so I was able to buy clothes very cheaply for school. I loved being well dressed in high school and college. Second, the pay was actually decent. My job was to deliver packages to customers (usually lawyers and doctors) at their downtown offices, all of which were walking distance from the store. I made good tips and got to meet a lot of different people. When I graduated from high school, Davison's made it very easy for me to get a credit card!

» *Playing Hooky*

Starting in eleventh grade, one of my fast friends had the bright idea that we dress up in high-heeled shoes and stockings and pretend to be student teachers from Clark College, a nearby black college, rather than the high-school students we were. Booker T. was a big school, and the security guards so constantly turning over, so no one caught on to our ploy for the longest time. Students weren't allowed to leave campus, but student teachers most assuredly were; therefore, dressed like teachers, we skipped the cafeteria every day in favor of lunch at the corner drugstore near Morehouse, the local black men's college. The Morehouse boys knew to expect us, and they would come over and flirt with us for the fifteen or twenty minutes we could spare before class began again.

We almost got away with it too. It was baccalaureate Sunday, with all of us set to graduate high school, when one fatal flaw brought me literally to my knees in despair. We'd all arrived early at the city auditorium for graduation practice—so early that we thought we had time to leave, squeeze in a quick breakfast, and make it back before anyone noticed we were gone. We were late returning, though, and the principal saw us sneak in. He was debating whether to even let us come to baccalaureate when one of the security guards who'd seen us leave every day at lunch wandered over. "Those girls?" the guard exclaimed. "You mean they're our high-school students?" He then told how we'd presented ourselves to him as student teachers from Clark College.

Knowing the game was up, when the principal asked us whether the guard's story was true, I got down on my knees and drew on everything I'd ever learned in drama class. "Please, Principal Carnell," I wailed. "Please forgive us! Sometimes we *would* go over to Yates and Milton Drug Store to eat lunch, and we *would* get back late, but we're *sorry!*" Prostrate, I prayed and cried hysterically. What would our parents say if their kids couldn't even be at their own service?

Principal Carnell said, "Go home. I need to think about this. I'll call each of you around four or four thirty to let you know whether you can march at six." We went home, nervous wrecks, but he finally called and let us walk.

» Meeting W. E. B. Du Bois

William Edward Burghardt (W. E. B.) Du Bois (1868–1963) was one of the greatest black leaders who ever lived. The first African American to earn a doctorate from Harvard, Du Bois became an economics professor at Atlanta University, where he inspired countless classes of students to activism and recruited many more for the National Association for the Advancement of Colored People (NAACP), which he cofounded in 1909.

As a high-school junior, I'd heard of Du Bois and his work but really only knew the superficial stuff that made the occasional newspaper headline. That's why, when our English teacher assigned us to pick one black leader from Atlanta and interview him or her, I chose Du Bois; I was intrigued by him and wanted to learn more. I didn't bother doing any in-depth research to prepare, so consequently I was nervous and embarrassed during our interview and quickly ran out of questions. As I recall, Du Bois took pity on me and didn't harangue me for wasting his time, which would have been his right. Instead, he escorted me to his working room and handed me copies of some books that he'd written from which to pull information for my report. It wasn't until the following year that my ineptitude came back to haunt me.

In twelfth grade, Mrs. L. D. Shivery was my homeroom teacher, and she was an excellent one at that. The story around campus was that whenever someone called her at school, she answered the phone by saying, "This is Mrs. L. D. Shivery, would-be principal of Booker T. Washington High were I not a woman." Mrs. Shivery wanted to give us a real-world education and not just a textbook one, meaning that she lectured about timely and relevant topics with immediate applications to our lives. I remember her warning: "If any of your fathers work for contractors and wear those dirty clothes, tell them that they need to keep some nice clothes in a bag, and when they get off work, to go change—so they look like proud men, and not some dirty worker getting on the bus." She impressed on us the importance of appearance and of self-worth. "These are tricks," she would say, "for beating The System." The world never knew what those black teachers in the 1930s and 1940s were doing for America's black students; miracle workers, they were.

Well, it so happened that Mrs. Shivery was also the official hostess for Dr. Du Bois in Atlanta. He was not married, and she was a widow. (Her husband had committed suicide.) One day, she said, "Guess what, students? Some dumb English teacher at this school sent some bushy red-haired student who didn't know anything to interview the great Dr. Du Bois." She had no idea the student had been me, but everyone else did, and they were rolling on the floor laughing. Even I thought it was hilarious. I could whoop and holler with the best of them because I had met W. E. B. Du Bois and had been forever changed and humbled by the experience. That meeting formed and informed my sense of personal responsibility for tackling the black situation in America head-on.

» *Other Formative Experiences from a Georgia Childhood*

When I was thirteen or fourteen, I was invited to spend Christmas with a friend in a small town outside Atlanta. Her parents knew my parents, so over the holidays we went from house to house with her friends and had so much fun. I'd never been to so many parties. By the time I left, her friends were my friends, and they all came down to see me off on the bus back to Atlanta.

Now, even though Atlanta was segregated, it was far and away the most liberal of Georgia's cities—certainly more forward-thinking than the tiny town in which my new friends lived. When the bus pulled up, I knew to go sit on the back bench for blacks, but I didn't know about any kind of boarding order. I jumped up on that bus step, turned around, and waved a grand good-bye to the girls, only to be promptly scolded by the white bus driver: "Where you think you goin', nigger?" I was shocked and replied, "To Atlanta." He answered, "Not before white folks, you don't." He pushed me off the bus in front of all my friends, saying, "Stand and wait there." I was so embarrassed that I cried my heart out, and I didn't get on a commercial bus again for more than fifty years. I never thought I was better than anybody else, but I also didn't think that anyone was better than I was. Society kept on telling me that's how it was, though.

No one was going to stop me from exercising my democratic right to vote, however. Georgia was one of the first states to lower the voting age from twenty-one to eighteen in 1943. Although technically I wouldn't turn eighteen until 1947, remember that I had the legal paperwork to pass as eighteen (and was indeed living as an eighteen-year-old) in 1945. By then I was living with Aunt Ida in Atlanta, but I registered to vote under my old address in Bagley Park so I could vote in that precinct's election. Everyone warned me not to bother; they all feared harm if they attempted to vote. And maybe it would have been an issue if we'd all blown in as a big group. Instead I walked into that booth by myself, the only black in the room, I voted, and it counted. White people stared at me as though they wanted to ask, *What are you doing here?* Their silent gazes could not overpower a young black woman with a voice, however.

Later on, I could not get a driver's license in Georgia. You first had to secure a permit to take driving lessons, and then you could be licensed if you passed the test. One day I went down to the Atlanta office in which the permits were issued. I was told to get in line. The officer handing out the permits said, "Your line is over there." I understood that I had been assigned to the black line, which was on the other side of the room from the white line. The officer sat at a desk at the head of and in between the two lines. He worked fairly, alternately calling up a white and then a black to fill out their paperwork for a permit. What I objected to was how the officer addressed whites as "Mister" and "Missus," but called blacks by saying, "Boy (or girl), you're next." We were never respected as women and men.

On my turn, the officer said, "Girl, you're next." I accepted my permit and then said, "You know what? That's not right for you to call us 'boys' and 'girls.'" He jumped up and grabbed that permit back from me so fast I didn't have a chance. "When you learn to act ladylike, you can come back and get your permit," he said. "How can I be a lady if I'm not treated as such?" I retorted. I didn't learn to drive until I moved to Texas, because I wasn't going back to those divided-up lines, where I was called a girl even though I'd graduated from college and was a full-grown woman.

» *The Spelman Years*

Despite the bad influence of my friends, I ultimately excelled in high school. Grade point averages weren't being used yet; instead of a 4.0 you earned a percentage, 1–100. My average at graduation was 87 percent, a B+. It won me a full four-year scholarship to Spelman College, an elite black women's college in Atlanta (and counterpart to Morehouse).

In 2016, *US News and World Report* ranked Spelman College as the number one HBCU (historically black college or university) and seventy-second-overall-best liberal arts school.[*] In addition to graduating countless notable authors, artists, actresses, educators, executives, and even the first black female to obtain the rank of general in the United States Air Force, Spelman has graduated more African American women judges than any other university in the country. Included among their ranks are Romae Powell, a great advocate for juvenile justice whose legacy in Atlanta is the Judge Romae T. Powell Juvenile Justice Center, and Bernette Johnson, chief justice of the Louisiana Supreme Court. Michelle Obama has been a graduation speaker at Spelman, and the school is often known as the Radcliffe or Wellesley of the African American world. It means something to earn a Spelman degree—especially when your own mother never made it past elementary school.

But then that was the whole point of Spelman's mission: to give women of African descent opportunities that their forebears didn't have. In 1881, two teachers and missionaries named Harriet Giles and Sophia Packard founded what was then called the Atlanta Baptist

---

[*] http://colleges.usnews.rankingsandreviews.com/best-colleges/spelman-college-141060/overall-rankings.

Female Seminary to educate newly freed women and their daughters. The following year, Giles and Packard were campaigning for funds when they were introduced to wealthy northern Baptist businessman John D. Rockefeller at a church conference in Ohio. So impressed was Rockefeller with their vision that the abolitionist-leaning magnate gave them the last $200 in his pocket and informed them he would stay in touch. He later settled the debt on the seminary's property and funded the building of Rockefeller Hall, at which point the school was renamed Spelman Seminary after Rockefeller's wife, whose parents were Harvey and Lucy Henry Spelman. Thereafter, one Rockefeller or another always sat on the board of trustees, and today students still attend Sisters Chapel, named for Mrs. Rockefeller and her sister.

Here's a story about that chapel: It used to be that we had to go to chapel every morning at 8:00 a.m. If I was staying with the Brittons, that was all right, but when I was visiting my mother, I had to catch a bus by 7:00 a.m. to get downtown on time. It's still dark at that hour during the winter, and in humid Georgia it rained frequently. On one such dark and rainy morning, I was walking to the bus stop when a beautiful, long, black car pulled up next to me. You'll remember that Buckhead was affluent, so the car was not necessarily out of place, and I'm sure the man inside it had nothing but the purest of intentions. Rolling down the window, he called, "Young lady, where are you going in all this rain?" When I told him, he said, "Why don't you jump in? I'll take you to the bus stop." Call it stranger danger, or just self-awareness; either way, I knew he was white and I was black, and I didn't like the situation. I said, "Thank you, sir, but I think I'll just walk on. I don't care about the rain, it's not bothering me that much." He acquiesced and drove off.

When I got to school that morning, I approached a white professor of religious studies whom I was very fond of. Admittedly embellishing the story a bit, I told him about my "terrible" experience in which "a white man stopped me and tried to make me get into his car. I was too scared," I concluded, "so I ran off." That man had not tried to abduct me, of course, but the concerned teacher said he would look into it. He ended up convincing the college president that it was "too dangerous" for me to be coming to school at that early hour, and she excused me from chapel for the rest of the winter semester. My friends chided me to no end, but they were just jealous.

» *History and Government*

At nearby Morehouse, I met my very first boyfriend: Arnold Cameron, a Kappa frat boy. I knew he was Kappa because one day when we were out walking around campus, I put my arm around his waist and felt a bundle of newspapers shoved down the back of his pants. Of course I questioned him, and he said it was padding for protection against his fraternity brothers, as he was to be hazed and beaten that night.

Arnold and I almost got married. He was a couple years older than I was and set to graduate soon. When I was leaving the drugstore one afternoon, I ran into Dr. Tilman, a professor of English at both Spelman and Morehouse. Dr. Tilman asked whether he had heard right—was I really going to marry Mr. Cameron? "The best thing you can do," he said, "is finish your education and get your degree." He continued: "A man may like to look at a pretty face across the table when he eats breakfast or dinner, but he will soon get bored if his mate can't contribute to conversations. Women should be intellectually equal to men." Call Dr. Tilman an early feminist, but his advice was the right advice. Arnold went on to become an alcoholic social worker in California who was later killed by his own son.

Several of the girls I'd run with in high school matriculated at Spelman as well, but most of them didn't last very long. Like me, they were too concerned with the men's basketball games and track meets next door, and they all woke up one morning and had Fs in psychology. Even I was barely squeaking by with a D at the time. (I'd been turning in an assignment here and there but really doing just enough to get by.) We decided to send the most attractive one among us to do a little wheeling and dealing with the psychology professor. It wasn't about sex necessarily; we just wanted to give him some encouragement to at least give us passing grades. What we didn't realize is that you can't "out-psychology" a psychologist, because he sees right through you. I ended up owning that D; the rest of the girls flunked out.

My negligence caused me to lose my scholarship. That was the turning point for me—no more coasting; it was time to get down to business. Originally, I had wanted to be a math major, but that degree was available only through Morehouse. The president of Spelman at the time was a white woman who felt that freshman ladies did not have the maturity to attend Morehouse, that we would end up pregnant or worse. Only as juniors and seniors were Spelman students allowed to take Morehouse classes, but by then I had forgotten most of the math I once knew. Besides, it was too much work to start a major that late in the game. That's how I wound up with a bachelor's degree in history and government.

» *The Black Renaissance*

A black woman who finished not only high school but also college was in uncharted territory in a lot of ways; most of my classmates had dropped out after that year spent planting flowers in seventh grade. Kids were tired of catching the bus, school seemed a drag, and classes didn't make you money—at first anyway. Decades later at my high-school class reunion, I would recognize only one person from the elementary school I attended who went on to do anything with her life. Had it not been for my academic record and the Brittons's encouragement, I probably wouldn't have gone to college either, but I was determined to make something of myself. My perseverance is what made me stand out, and it's the reason my first job post-Spelman was literally handed to me.

Mrs. Perry, a black professional woman, worked for the Fulton County school district as a liaison between it and the Buckhead black community. She'd known me since I was in grade school and had kept tabs on me over the years. As soon as I graduated college, she offered me a teaching position with the county—no tests, certifications, or interviews required. I started teaching third grade and was immediately overwhelmed. Without a single education credit to my name, I knew nothing of curriculum development, pedagogy, or classroom management. Teaching smart kids was easy enough, but what to do with all the dumb or ill-behaved ones? For a while, I tried paying the smart students to help me tutor their peers, and then when I couldn't stand it any longer, I switched to ninth grade.

I wasn't much better with the older kids, but I gave myself small consolations. Enjoying an income for the very first time, I splurged on a real fur cape from Davison's. It cost me forty-seven dollars a month to pay off, but it proudly replaced the faux fur cape my aunt had gifted me in college. I used to wear her cape to church on Sun-

As a young woman

days until the other students teased me about not getting it wet in the rain. "It's not real," they taunted, "and it's going to look terrible!" No one could make fun of my Davison's cape.

Still, something had to be done about my (absent) teaching skills, so during summer vacations I began taking classes at Atlanta University (where Du Bois was teaching) toward a master's degree in political science. I had taken an interest in politics in Atlanta, so I thought getting a master's degree in political science was the right choice. Atlanta was on the same general campus as Clark, Spelman, and Morehouse, meaning there was a large concentration of powerful leaders in one place. In many ways, that quadrangle became the hub of a new Black Renaissance. I remember going to listen to Benjamin Mays, then the president of Morehouse, speak about confronting racial discrimination without pandering to it. He used as a symbol the Fox Theater, a segregated movie theater in downtown Atlanta. Blacks could attend, but they had to sit in the upstairs balcony—derogatorily called the Buzzard Roost—and to reach the balcony, they had to walk up a rickety set of stairs on the building's exterior.* I used to go on dates there with my beaus, and if any of us made too much noise, we'd be told by the management, "Quiet down; you're disturbing the white folks!" To Mays, the idea that we would pay money to be segregated was entirely self-defeating. Mays was president of Morehouse when M. L. was a student there; he likely influenced many of the reverend's early views.

Then there was Whitney Young, founder of the National Urban League. He taught social work at Atlanta University, and I always saw him around. John Wesley Dobbs, a black activist, president of the black Masons, and leader of the Republican Party in Georgia, had several daughters who attended Spelman; I met him when I was fundraising contributions for the school's yearbook. I also met Dobbs's grandson, Maynard Jackson, who would become Atlanta's first African American mayor. William Boyd, another professor at Atlanta University, became the state president of the NAACP. Jesse Blayton taught business at Morehouse, organized the first Mutual Federal Savings and Loan Association, and, with his partners Clayton Yates and Lorimer Milton, formed a coalition to run Citizens Trust Bank, which Milton had been instrumental in establishing and Yates had helped to save from financial collapse. The list goes on, but suffice it to say I was drinking from the fountain of the movement! After coming into contact with all these great black leaders, there was no turning back for me.

---

*Every rule has an exception. I once saw a black woman accompany a white child into the main theater. Because the woman was the child's maid and caretaker, it was considered all right for the black maid to sit where the white people sat.

» *Mitchell versus UGA*

The more politically aware I became, the more civic minded I grew, and I soon joined up with the NAACP in Atlanta. No one need question my commitment to The Struggle after that defining experience. Hearing M. L. had opened my eyes to black civil rights; interviewing NAACP founder W. E. B. Du Bois in high school had impressed on me the power of black leadership; and working side by side with the NAACP—which I became a member of the Board of—stoked a slowly growing fire to become not just a good citizen of the world but also a responsible one, actively advocating for change and a new world (re)order. I realized the best way to shape hearts and minds was at the source: America's children.

Newly rededicated to the privilege of teaching, I decided to pursue a teaching certificate, which I hoped would bolster my woeful skills and help to identify and arm me with a powerhouse pedagogy for social reform.

At the time, the best teaching-certification program in Georgia was offered by the University of Georgia (UGA). I could not attend UGA, however, because Georgia's white state colleges and universities were not open to blacks. Precedent had been set for black plaintiffs to bring before the court cases that could contest the separate-but-equal-facilities provision of *Plessy v. Ferguson* by proving that there *were* in fact no equal facilities, not when it came to certain educational programming, at least. Since legal action wasn't immediately available to me, I took the next best avenue: appealing to UGA's chancellor in person. I'd heard about other blacks across the South who were being paid to go out of state. Basically, if we had a right to equal, albeit separate, facilities and the state could not (or would not) provide such a facility, then they were required to compensate us by whatever means necessary via access to an equal facility *somewhere*.

Brandishing my acceptance letter to Columbia University's teaching-certification program in New York, I explained to the chancellor how I would prefer to attend UGA, but if he wouldn't take my money, then Columbia it would be—on a couple of conditions.

"First," I said, "UGA's courses cost twenty-five dollars per credit hour, but Columbia's cost seventy-five dollars per credit hour. I can't afford that."

"We'll pay the fifty dollars per credit hour difference for you to go to Columbia," he said.

"Okay," I said. "What about transportation? I could drive from Atlanta to Athens and the gas would not cost that much. But I'll have to take a train to New York."

He said, "We'll take care of that too."

"Fine, but there's another thing. In Athens, I could stay with relatives for free. New York is a very expensive place to live."

"We'll work out a stipend for your residence in New York," he agreed.

"That sounds all right then," I told him. As I made to leave, I added, "By the way, my friend Carrie Clements is sitting out there in the lobby, and she's registered for Columbia too."

He sighed. "We'll pay for her too."

I ran out into the lobby laughing, grabbed my girlfriend, who'd gotten cold feet at the last minute, and skipped out into the Georgia sunshine. That, folks, was how you worked a system designed to oppress you—or so I thought.

» *Thurgood to the Rescue*

Carrie Clements (now Dr. Carrie Johnson) and I moved to New York that summer, trading the hot metropolis of Atlanta for the infinitely more sophisticated Big Apple. It was the first time out of state for both of us, and we really thought we'd made it—two young and single women-about-town. First thing, we went to Columbia to sign up for classes, and how flippantly did I toss out an "Oh, Georgia will send you a check to cover tuition"! The administrator looked both annoyed and amused when he said, "You realize you won't get that check until after you've completed your course work, right?" I must've flashed those deer-in-headlights eyes, because he said more gently, "It's a reimbursement, dear, not a disbursement."

You can bet my world collapsed a bit right then. I'd planned for three months of mostly funded fun before classes started in September, and all of a sudden I was homeless, jobless, and rather penniless. In a last-ditch effort to find a work-around, I decided to call in the big guns. Having read about a young black man named Thurgood Marshall, who, as the defense lawyer for the NAACP, had filed suit over Horace Ward (another young black man) being unable to matriculate at the University of Georgia, I thought Thurgood might be able to help me as well. Thus, dressed to kill, I showed up unannounced one day at the national office of the NAACP.

Pretending like I knew what I was doing, I shared an elevator ride to the proper floor with a tall, handsome black man just a few years older than I was. Shyly, I asked whether he knew where I could find Mr. Marshall. "I do," he said. "Follow me." The man led me to the right office and then turned around and asked, "Now, what may I do for you?" I was talking to Thurgood himself! Quickly, I spilled my story. I asked to become a plaintiff in my own suit to enter the University of Georgia. "Barring that," I asked, "could I be added to the suit for Horace Ward?" While Thurgood commiserated, in the end there was nothing he could do.* He suggested that Carrie and I limit our expenses as much as possible and that we find part-time jobs in the meantime.

Defeated, Carrie and I moved to the least expensive (still not exactly affordable) section of the city, which at the time was Harlem. We continued looking for an apartment closer to campus, only to realize that even New York had its bigots. Despite their clearly displayed vacancy signs, no one could find a room for two black women. Eventually we were able to move, but we were still far enough away that we had to bus to campus.

---

*Horace Ward's case was never resolved in court. Ward finally entered Northwestern University and ultimately became a federal judge. Just two years ago, I saw Ward at the National Bar Association convention and heard that UGA had bestowed on him an honorary doctorate in recognition of the groundwork he laid toward desegregation. Thurgood Marshall, of course, went on to become the first African American justice of the United States Supreme Court! Later, as chair of the media committee of the Atlanta NAACP, I became the fortunate driver to transport Thurgood Marshall to press conferences and other events on his visits.

» *Johns Hopkins University (JHU) Fellowship*

At Columbia, I took enough credit hours to comply with the law for certification in Georgia, and I applied myself to them diligently. In addition to two or three academic classes, we took a couple of education electives that could be on any topic. I loved to play golf, so I took golf for a whole semester in New York. It actually came in very handy a few years down the road, but more on that later.

I was still a student at Columbia in 1954, pursuing the teaching certification while finishing my master's degree by correspondence from Atlanta. That spring I graduated simultaneously from Atlanta University's political science program and Columbia's teaching program, and I immediately landed a summer-long fellowship at the Johns Hopkins University School of International Relations in Washington, DC. Part of the reason I made for such an attractive applicant was that my master's thesis on the republic of Israel had just received a newsworthy commendation from the Israeli embassy in New York City.* For six weeks, I took two more courses at JHU, one on French Africa and one on political geography, or the role that geography plays in international relations (think the present-day Israeli-Palestinian conflict). The paper I produced on the development of nationalism in Morocco

---

*When I went in person to receive this commendation, the embassy's director was understandably curious as to why a young black woman had chosen to write about Israel, of all places. I explained how at Spelman College I had first become aware of the Jewish contributions to the early civil rights movement. Not only did a Jewish professor named Joel Spingarn serve on the national board of the NAACP, but Arthur Schomburg, a Jewish scholar and bibliophile, established Harlem's Schomburg Center for Research in Black Culture. I was so amazed at these revelations that when it later came time to write my master's thesis, I selected Israel as the subject so the world would know that black people appreciated the role that Jews played in our lives.

was subsequently published in *Phylon*, Atlanta University's scholarly journal.

The amazing thing about the French Africa class was that there were actual African students in it as well as African American students and some whites. Kofi Prempeh, a member of the Ghanaian royal family, was enrolled at JHU, and we became friends. When Ghana gained its independence from England in 1957, Kofi's wealthy family offered to buy me a plane ticket to travel to their country and participate in the celebrations. Just before the first president's inauguration, however, Kofi was assassinated. I was sad for him and his family and even more disappointed that I didn't get to go to Ghana.

Before I finished the fellowship at JHU, I briefly thought about finding some way to stay on the East Coast awhile longer. With my background in government, political science, and now international relations, I figured I must qualify for a job with the state department. The day I wandered downtown to register for the foreign civil-service exam, I saw an African American official at the embassy's desk. I told him I was interested in sitting for the exam and asked him why so few foreign-service officers were black. He explained that it was up to the department head to choose one out of the three top-scoring applicants and that the department head tended to pick the applicant who came from his own alma mater (if there was one) or at the very least from an Ivy League. Given that schools like Harvard and Yale enrolled far fewer black students than traditional HBCUs, the odds of a minority applicant making the cut just weren't great. I relinquished that idea and just enjoyed the remainder of my time at JHU.

On my last weekend in Washington DC, I gave a party for the whole JHU student body. I was living in a downtown apartment then occupied mostly by other black scholars and businesspeople. It just so happened that the unit across the hall from me was empty. I got the manager's permission to have the party there. A friend's boyfriend worked as a rep for one of the big liquor companies. He generously supplied all the leftover alcohol from their last event. Someone else knew a local band who would play music for free. I just had to provide the hors d'oeuvres, which was hardly a problem seeing as the fellowship money covered all my other expenses that summer. In addition to students and professors (who came because they'd "heard blacks had great times on Saturday nights"), I invited several of the diplomats I'd met through the fellowship program. The party was so successful that it snagged a write-up in *JET* magazine. It was the best way to end my time there, for sure.

» *The Year of Benjamin Brown*

September 1954 found me back in Atlanta and putting to good use the teacher certification I'd just earned in New York. I picked up right where I'd left off with Fulton High's ninth grade. Carrie came back too, and she started teaching at the same school. To fill my hours outside the classroom, I joined the Atlanta NAACP. I served on the board of the women's auxiliary, a group that spent many hours registering voters and getting them to the polls. Our chair was Geneva Haugabrooks, director of Haugabrooks Funeral Home. Today, former Georgia state representative Lottie Watkins and I are (as far as I know) the only survivors of that important group.

The year 1954 was the year of Benjamin Brown, a story I love to tell because Ben is so special to me, and I'm so proud of everything he accomplished. Benjamin Brown was a student in a ninth-grade class that I taught; he was a very smart student. I think he was very impressed with me. He became my student leader, encouraging other students to vote at eighteen years of age. He went on to College Park and organized a youth NAACP chapter. I had already moved away when he graduated from high school. Ben went to Clark and soon became a legislator and then assistant to President Carter. I was always so proud of him that every now and then, when he was in college, I would send him a money order to show him how proud I was of him.

It all started when Ben and I discovered a mutual love of golfing. In those days, golf was not a sport available to black high-school students in Atlanta, so Ben and I teamed up to campaign to bring golf to Fulton County's black students. We began by attending a city council meeting and presenting on the need for and benefits of access to a student golfing facility. Amazingly, the council agreed and offered to sponsor a golf tournament at Atlanta's only black golf course. Ben organized all the Fulton High boys (girls weren't allowed—yet) and contacted other area schools about competing against us. I loaned the boys my own set of clubs to practice with, and do you know what? I never saw those clubs again!

At the end of that school year, Benjamin helped me plan a house party for all the student golfers to celebrate the success of our spring tournament. I remember that in the middle of the party, I had to run to the store to get something, and my grandfather, the minister, just happened to stop by. He had an absolute fit that all those kids were in my house unattended, but no harm came of it. Subsequently, parents of some of the boys who had worked as caddies organized a legitimate golf organization for the students, and I was relieved of that duty.

Ben Brown's and my story did not end there, however. On his graduation, Ben joined in my work with the Atlanta NAACP. We started an NAACP youth chapter together in College Park, which Ben went on to lead. We then focused on the black vote, registering to vote as many eighteen-year-old high-school students as we could.

Ultimately, these early experiences prepared Ben to become a wildly successful Georgia politician. After graduating from college, he served in the Georgia House of Representatives in 1966 and again from 1969–1977. He was the first chairman of the Georgia Legislative Black Caucus. Ben resigned from the legislature in 1977 to accept a position in President Carter's administration. I followed Ben's career all the while, staying in touch when I could, and when Carter later hosted a luncheon for black educational leaders from across the country, Ben didn't forget me. He secured for me, a humble teacher among all those elite college presidents, an invitation to the White House! I rode up the elevator with Benjamin and Jimmy Carter himself, grinning from ear to ear and proud beyond words of the man that fourteen-year-old boy had become. Benjamin Brown was one of the highlights of my teaching career, a miracle whom I had the honor to help shape. He died in 1999.

I taught at Fulton High for only a few years during that second go-round with the school. Then Carrie convinced me to apply with her to Southern University at Baton Rouge, and both of us were hired on the spot. Carrie taught business, and I taught government and geography for two years. During that time, I chartered an alumnae chapter for Spelman College, which is still active today.

From there, Carrie went on to earn her PhD from SUNY Buffalo. I applied and was accepted to teach at Prairie View A&M University, an HBCU in the Texas A&M system, about forty-five miles northwest of Houston. Moving to Texas was a good decision. While at Prairie View, I was able to take some of my students to hear Congressman Adam Clayton Powell, a great civil rights leader, speak at Texas Southern University. As pastor of Harlem's Abyssinian Baptist Church (the largest African American church in New York City), Powell once directed his parishioners who were being mistreated by a telephone service provider to pay their bills in pennies. Needless to say, once the company began fielding pound after pound of pennies, they quickly started treating their customers better.

PART II » EARLY CAREER

But what of black women? I most sincerely doubt if any other race of women could have brought its fineness up through so devilish a fire.
—W. E. B. DU BOIS

» *An Evening with MLK Jr.*

One spring in the late 1950s, my Houston girlfriends called to let me know that Martin Luther King Jr. (M. L.) would be giving the commencement speech at a black business school. Eleanor Allen would be hosting him for dinner, and did I care to join? Eleanor, I should add, was married to Dr. Andrew Arthur Allen, a well-to-do orthodontist and the father of Debbie Allen and Phylicia Rashad (who wrote the foreword for this book). Eleanor had a gorgeous house, and her spread was sure to be a beautiful one, so of course I wanted to go. I also hadn't seen M. L. for at least a year, back when we had both shown up in Nashville for unrelated reasons. He had attended the Institute of Race Relations at Fisk University in 1956 and just happened to stay overnight with his dear friend Dr. Wilmateen Jackson, who was also my best friend and whom I was in Nashville visiting at the time. We'd all stayed up late talking and laughing.

The night of M. L.'s reception at Eleanor's house, it fell to me to pick him up from his hotel, even though the girls always teased me about being a bad driver. After I had him in the car, I asked him, "Do you mind if we stop by my seamstress's house? I need to pick up a dress that she's making me for Easter. She's making me a hat to match it." (I'm known for wearing hats.) He said, "Of course, Harriet, stop wherever you want to stop." We stopped at her house, and I rang the doorbell. When the seamstress answered, I grandly announced, "Mrs. D., I would like for you to meet the Reverend Dr. Martin Luther King Jr." I'm sure she was quite polite about it all, asking M. L. to take a seat while we went to the sewing room. Once we were out of earshot, however, she exclaimed, "Oh my Lord! That's Dr. Martin Luther King sitting in my living room! Oh, what am I going to do?" I didn't understand and asked her to clarify. "Well," she said, "how am I gonna let people know that Dr. Martin Luther King is at my house?

A young Hugh Allen, son of Eleanor Allen, with Martin Luther King Jr.

Can I call a neighbor to come down and verify that he's here?" Embarrassed, I told her I would speak with him.

M. L. was always so kind and gracious and down-to-earth. When I explained to him why Mrs. D. wanted to invite a friend over, he said he didn't mind at all. That's the funniest story I have about M. L. and the only personal one from after the time he became famous. We did eventually make it to Eleanor's dinner. The next day, we girls went to hear his speech at the business school.

» Mitchell, Meet Moore

A year or two later, in 1959, I met and married my first husband, Dr. Obrey Jesus (O. J.) Moore. O. J. was significantly older than I was (I was thirty-two), but he was a physician in good standing, and he was wealthy. He owned a hospital and clinic called Camp Normal on Main Street in Longview. We met at Prairie View's health conference for black Texas physicians. A girlfriend named Emma and I had been invited to the conference reception simply because we were single. (It was well understood that the opening reception was a mixer of sorts, meant to meet your date.) I spotted O. J. almost immediately, and Emma, too, met a doctor that night. We all relocated to another Prairie View professor's house for a nightcap, and then O. J. and I sat in his car and talked until the wee hours of the morning. When he dropped me off at the dormitory later, he asked whether he could see me again. Soon enough, we were married.

Emma never did get married, although we had plenty of high times with the black officers from Fort Hood who used to visit Prairie View. Today, Emma is the very well-loved Fulton County commissioner, an office that her supporters say she will fill until she dies, so sensitive is she to the needs of the people in her constituency. In her precinct, she built one of the finest senior housing facilities I've ever seen and named it The Harriet G. Darnell Senior Multipurpose Facility after her mother, a church leader who was equally active in community affairs. I finally stopped asking her why she's never gotten married.

It's the truth that in high school, my fast girlfriends and I always talked about how we were going to marry rich men. One girlfriend married a dentist in Houston, and Eleanor, of course, married Dr. Allen. Another married a grocery-store owner, and a fourth married a military officer. When I married O. J. and moved with him to

Longview, Texas, we all felt as though we'd achieved what we'd said we would.

It didn't take long for this headstrong woman to realize that security, too, has a price. As it turned out, O. J. and I frequently didn't see eye to eye. He already had a child from a previous marriage and didn't want any more. Worse, though, was that he didn't think his wife should work. Due to my continuing NAACP activism, I'd begun to entertain thoughts of law school, but when I shared these, O. J. said, "I didn't marry a lawyer; I married a housewife." More than just protective, he was controlling, to the point that when the social studies teacher at a Longview school left and they asked me to temporarily fill in, I had to get O. J.'s permission first. Me, who'd learned and lectured around the country!

One day I called up Doris Hall, Eleanor's sister, and confessed, "Sometimes I wonder whether it's better to have security or freedom." It seemed to me then as though a woman couldn't have both. I'd opted for security, but at what cost? Daunted and cowed, I swept my law school dreams into a dark corner and never mentioned them to O. J. again.

» *The Civil Rights Act of 1964 and More NAACP*

To occupy the long and lonely days, I threw myself even more into local volunteerism. Particularly interesting was the year I spent "testing" the Civil Rights Act of 1964. The Civil Rights Act outlawed discrimination based on race, color, religion, sex, or national origin, and it effectively ended racial segregation in public facilities.

But the law wasn't always enforced, at least not at first—so I made it a personal mission of mine to out any Longview restaurants that refused to serve me. Another black housewife by the name of Mrs. White and I went restaurant to restaurant that summer, enjoying many good meals while standing up for black citizens everywhere. At the very first restaurant we went to, the manager would not seat us until he called and got the "approval" of the richest white woman in the county. "There are two Negroes here who want to be served under the '64 law," I heard him tell her. She must have given him the go-ahead, because we were served all right. Once word got around about what we were doing, other restaurant owners acquiesced with a sigh, saying, "Since everyone else is doing it, we'll do it too."

Having crossed restaurants off our list, we next tackled Longview's other important public facilities, such as the courthouse. Of all the places to openly flout a law, you'd think a court of law would have a bit more self-respect. Instead, the building kept its designated "Colored" signs above the water fountains until I called the Justice Department. They sent someone to take the signs down, but can you imagine? Clearly, discrimination was alive and well in east Texas. That's why I stayed active with the NAACP. As I'd done in Atlanta, I again advocated for voter registration in Longview. A team of high-school students and I got blacks registered to vote and got them to the polls. We increased voter turnout in Gregg County from 15 percent to 25 percent. As a result, I received an invitation to Lyndon Baines Johnson's inauguration in 1965.*

One other achievement of note during my years on the NAACP board was securing Barbara Jordan as a speaker at one of our annual dinners. Jordan, a black Democrat, was the first African American elected to the Texas Senate after Reconstruction. I'd heard her speak previously and knew what a dynamic presenter she was. Amazingly, she accepted our invitation, and she even stayed with O. J. and me during her one night in town. In her address, she applauded the work of Dr. Lonnie Smith, a black dentist from Houston's fifth ward. Smith had sued the county's elected officials for the right to vote in the Democratic primary election, challenging the 1923 state law that required all voters to be white. Prior to *Smith v. Allwright*, blacks in Texas could vote on election day but not in the primary, and if you couldn't vote in the primary, you had no effect on the election.

The second person I invited to speak at the second annual dinner was LeRoy Johnson, the first black Georgia senator following Reconstruction. I thought he would be a great inspiration. Senator Johnson was also responsible, along with Jesse Hill, who was president of the Atlanta YMCA, for convincing the mayor of Atlanta to give a permit to let Mohammed Ali fight in the United States again. He had not been able to get a permit to box in America after fighting in Africa.

---

*Barack Obama is great, but Lyndon Baines Johnson remains my favorite US president. In addition to passing the Civil Rights Act and the Voting Rights Act, introducing Medicare, and tackling the War on Poverty, he asked Hollywood to put more black extras in street scenes so the American public could get accustomed to seeing them. He also appointed Thurgood Marshall to the Supreme Court.

» O. J.'s Death

Although I'd shoved thoughts of law school to the back of a high shelf, I never wavered in my conviction that *someone* had to champion black rights in east Texas and that someone could be me—deprecating husband or no. Five years after marrying O. J., my competing wishes for security and freedom were granted. No one saw the leukemia coming. By the time he was diagnosed, the disease was late stage, and O. J. refused to seek treatment at Good Shepherd Hospital in Longview, where his chances for survival might have been the best. But he would have been given a room in the Colored Ward. Despite practicing as a doctor, O. J. was too proud to check himself in as a patient at a segregated facility.*

The man publicly known as the treasure of the Texas Black Physicians Organization opted instead to go to Riverside Hospital, a black hospital in Houston.† By then, it was too late. In the wake of

---

*As a distinguished doctor in the state of Texas, O. J. could refer his white patients who were seriously ill to Good Shepherd, but he did not have the right to attend to them. He had to call white doctor friends to be their medical providers. It was President Johnson's (bless his heart!) Medicare legislation that finally desegregated hospitals throughout the South.

†Originally called the Houston Negro Hospital when it was dedicated in 1926, Riverside had an entirely black staff and was home to the first training facility for black nurses in Houston. When it was discovered there was a cyst in my uterus and I needed surgery, I too refused to be treated at Longview Hospital in the Colored Ward. I too chose to go to Riverside. My girlfriend, Eleanor Allen, did the same. She had a serious heart condition and wanted the best doctor in Houston to perform the vital surgery—Dr. Denton Cooley. He had recently performed the first heart transplant in the world. Dr. Cooley came to Riverside hospital in his van with his staff of nurses and technicians and performed Eleanor's successful surgery. She lived many years afterward.

O. J.'s death, I inherited his new white Cadillac and enough money to cover tuition. You can bet I left Longview without a backward glance, although I thought I'd return someday, better armed for the fight.

» *Law School at UT*

I understand as well as the next person the complicated reputation of the lawyer. Supposed sentries of the law, for every "good" lawyer it seems there are two corrupt attorneys out there practicing for the money rather than for the people. Popular opinion was hardly the only barrier to my becoming a lawyer, however. Race and gender lines were drawn on the judicial system in those days, and I had both working against me. Black and a female? It was a marvel that UT even admitted me.

On top of those distinct challenges, I harbored my own self-doubts—going all the way back to when I was thirteen years old. A deacon of the church one day asked me what I wanted to be when I grew up. I told him that I wanted to be a lawyer and that I would fight for black people. He said, "That's a good thing, Harriet, but lawyers don't make it into heaven." Right away I decided I'd rather go to heaven than be a lawyer. Later, I realized he was just one more man holding me back.

Doubt festers, though. At Spelman College, I worked for a time as a research assistant to an Atlanta University librarian named Dr. Lawrence Reddick. For fifteen dollars a month, I scoured the black papers looking for stories about black soldiers in World War II. Dr. Reddick wanted to write a book about them, so I cut out every article pertaining to buffalo soldiers and Tuskegee flyers. Of course, I read a lot of unrelated articles in the process (like those that offered my first glimpses of the Jewish contribution to the civil rights movement). One such article was about Benjamin Davis, a black lawyer in Atlanta. He had represented a communist labor leader named Angelo Herndon against the state, and in 1933, the South was desperate to quash anything resembling a labor movement. I read about how throughout the trial, Davis was referred to by the prosecutor as "that nigger lawyer" and how when the verdict was appealed, all mention of the word *nigger* was stricken from the record. I remember thinking I could never be a lawyer; I'd be crying all over the courtroom if that happened to me.

Somehow, I conquered my fears of the white legal system, I guess, or my pressing need for justice outweighed my fears. The first step was to take and pass the LSAT. Then, after consulting several white friends who had helped me in raising the black-voter turnout, I decided to apply to the University of Texas. According to them, it was the best school to go to if I was serious about returning to Gregg County. "There's no respect for Harvard here," they told me. Swallowing my pride over the fact that UT had only recently begun accepting black students, I applied and was admitted in the spring of 1966. My backup school had been Texas Southern, but I never did hear from them one way or another.

Wandering around campus for the first time after my acceptance, I recall being duly impressed by the law school and its faculty. Assistant Dean Gibson was particularly nice and agreed to let me defer until the summer semester. I matriculated as the single black student among the class of 1969 and became the only black student, period, for a time after Bertrain Christian graduated in the spring of 1967. (A few other black students enrolled in 1968.)

The very first thing I did was to trade in that white Cadillac I'd driven to Austin. The car was so long I couldn't easily parallel park it at UT. If I did manage to snag a parking space, often I'd have to wait for the cars around me to empty out just so I could back out of the parking lot. I quickly grew tired of that dance and exchanged the Cadillac for a Thunderbird: small, sleek, and sexy.

Then, to have a little income while I was a law student, I started teaching at nearby Huston-Tillotson College (now Huston-Tillotson University), another HBCU. Through the grapevine, I learned that Thurgood Marshall was coming to Austin on business, so I wrote and asked whether he would visit my classes. He was too busy for that, but we did squeeze in a friendly lunch, and it was great to see him

Here's a photo of me with Thurgood after he had retired from the Supreme Court. He was tall and handsome as a younger man.

again. I told him about Werdner Page Keeton, then the dean of the UT School of Law. I expressed my disappointment that Keeton had made no visible efforts to increase the number of black students at the law school. *Sweatt v. Painter* in 1950 had opened the UT law school to black applicants, but given the segregationist history of the school, few black students wanted to attend, even fifteen years later.

Thurgood's chiding was patient but to the point. "Dean Keeton and I are very good friends," he said. "I'm also a friend to his brother [who was teaching at Harvard]. You may not know it," Thurgood continued, "but Keeton has done a lot for us. He worked very hard with me on the case that opened the University of Oklahoma law school, and his brother helped too." I said I never knew that—no one had talked about Keeton's history prior to his coming to Austin. It changed my whole attitude toward the dean, who I thought cared nothing for helping African Americans advance.

I didn't know until I got to the university that there was only one black student at the law school. Then, I began to hear about the treatment. Naturally, as a political science major, I knew about *Sweatt v. Painter*, but law school was not really exciting to me. I did have the nerve to question professors where younger students didn't dare to. There was a constitutional law professor, Williams, who lectured on the wrong tactics that blacks were taking in using sit-ins, and I questioned him about it. My theory was that one of the main reasons for doing sit-ins was because they were the only way to do so, to fight for changes.

Because I am generally powerless to stand back and do nothing when I sense an opportunity for change, I began helping to recruit black students to UT's law school. As the only black student in the law school at that time, I joined a committee organized by Jim Boyle, a white student and my friend, to recruit black students to the law school. I must say, we had some real success. It's probably the thing I'm most proud of from my time at UT. Committee members served as ambassadors to Texas-area schools (including UT), interviewing interested seniors and sharing with them just why the UT law school was such a good option. We targeted the black schools, including Prairie View University and Jarvis Christian College in Hawkins, Texas. I had a friend in the administration at Jarvis who also helped recruit for us, and then we expanded outside the HBCUs as well. All told, we netted twelve or thirteen student recruits for the fall of 1968. One of them, Richard Scott, went on to become a judge and only recently retired as justice of the peace of Precinct 1. The precinct court is now named after him. Other notable names included Isaiah Hardy, Jasper Roe, Ivory Pollard, and Carnegie Mims. They were all males, but we still thought that was a pretty marvelous turnout.*

---

*When we weren't recruiting black law students to UT's law school, we joined UT's black undergraduate community to protest other important issues, such as UT's refusal to let black athletes try out for the school's football team.

» *Mitchell, Meet Murphy*

Between law school, teaching, and student recruitment, you'd think I'd have kept busy enough, but somehow I found the time to contend with gentlemen callers as well. As a physician, O. J. had been well connected in the community, and several of his Austin-based "friends" started circling protectively around my widowhood. Dr. Connor was particularly aggressive, always asking whether he could take me to dinner. Although he said he just wanted to look out for me, I had no intentions of marrying an older man again. Plus, like O. J., he was so set in his ways; he told me he'd never move from the house he had off Airport Boulevard, which was not a nice area of town then.

While I tried to balance being solicitous with not leading Dr. Connor on, in the end it was he who introduced me to my second husband, Pat Murphy. Connor had taken me to the first Alpha fraternity dance of the season in the fall of 1967, when across the floor I saw this tall, very handsome, quite light-skinned man who I couldn't take my eyes off of for the rest of the evening.

Come Monday morning, I called up a friend who taught physical education on campus and asked her just who the tall, handsome fella at the dance might have been. "Oh yeah, that was probably Pat Murphy," she said. "He's a local musician, plays the saxophone. In fact, I think he has a gig this Sunday. Wanna go?" She introduced me to Pat at the show, and he took me to dinner that night. I found out that Pat was a full-time postal worker (Austin's first black postal supervisor) and played with several bands around town on the weekends.

That was it; that was the beginning. Dr. Connor had to give up; Pat didn't leave him a choice. It used to be that, as Connor didn't cook and his wife was deceased, he ate dinner every evening at a black restaurant called The Georgian on 11th Street. Pat took to borrowing the Thunderbird, which he'd fallen in love with—perhaps even before falling in love with me—and would cruise in it unnecessarily slowly

Pat Murphy, musician

past The Georgian while Connor was having dinner. Soon enough, Pat broke up my relationship with Dr. Connor for good.

Our courtship elicited its own fair share of drama around campus. Not only was he one of the most eligible bachelors in town, but he looked downright white. A black maid at the law school kept me up on the gossip, saying one day she'd overheard a couple of faculty members in the lounge exclaim that "the only black student in the law school is getting ready to marry a white man!" I guess she set the record straight by telling them Pat was black.

Our wedding was simple. We were married in 1968 at a restaurant by a minister of the Church of Christ. I didn't wear a wedding dress, just a dressy dress. A couple of friends attended us. There was no honeymoon. Since my wedding to O. J. had also been simple (we married at O. J.'s house, with no one present but the preacher), I had wanted a bigger wedding in Longview when I married Pat. As with O. J. before him, though, I was again foiled by the man I married.

Even so (and I don't mean to compare my two husbands, but I think it's fair to say here), Pat gave me everything O. J. couldn't, or wouldn't. Pat supported my law career. He was there to put my first

Pat and I at one of the many social events we loved to attend.

robe on at my swearing-in as a judge. He never missed a day of work, either; we were partners in hard work that way.

We also adopted a child together. The first child we tried to adopt was a baby girl living in a facility that helped unwed mothers. To adopt a child there, all you had to do was repay however much the nonprofit had expended on that particular child. Our daughter was going to "cost" $900. Pat said he wasn't going to pay that much for a baby when his wife didn't have time for one anyway. I regret not forcing his hand, because when we finally did adopt, the experience was less than pleasant.

Our son, Charles, was twelve years old when we took him in. After only a short time, a psychiatrist suggested that Charles return to his natural parents since we were having so many problems with him. The doctor thought Charles would be more comfortable at "home," but home was the literal ghetto. Charles went on to father six children by different women. He married one of his baby mamas but abandoned her frequently. I helped her pursue a career in nursing. The six kids produced seven grandkids, and although I no longer claim Charles as my son, I claim all those kids and grandkids. Charles and I have never seen eye-to-eye and have had many differences.

Truth be told, though, I never gave Pat or the boy enough of my time. I was too involved with The Struggle. Juggling a family and two careers by that time, I failed at being a wife and mother. I can admit that now.

The other natural addition to a family is pets. Pat loved dogs, but I never liked them one bit. He liked to train them and take them to run around in the dog park. To my chagrin, we had three different dogs over the course of our marriage. I never stopped complaining until the day I read that pets are supposed to help people with heart conditions. Then I shut up until the last one died, but I didn't let Pat get another one. Probably my aversion stems from my mother and her cats. She used to feed them on the floor from the same bowls that we ate out of, which I found utterly unsavory.

But let's go back, for a moment, to law school.

» *One Last Bid for Change*

The last thing I did before graduating law school was to make an appointment with Dr. John Silber, then the dean of UT's College of Arts and Sciences, to ask him why he wasn't bringing black professors to campus. What exactly, I wanted to know, were his reasons for not hiring them? Silber regurgitated that tired line about being happy to hire black professors, if only he could find some. I can't tell you how many times I've heard that excuse in my life; when you ask upper management about hiring blacks, they say, "We just can't find one qualified." I then asked Dr. Silber about all the black PhDs that had graduated from UT. He said that UT had a policy about not hiring their own. To this day, I know there were qualified black professors out there, and I worry that I didn't try hard enough to change anything.

At least Dr. Silber got his comeuppance, though. Not too much later, Dr. Silber was fired by Regent Frank Erwin when Silber refused to help reorganize the College of Arts and Sciences. The College had grown too big, and it was determined that Silber's deanship gave one man too much power over too significant a portion of the student body. Naturally, Dr. Silber was loath to relinquish his position, so Regent Erwin relieved him of it. Dr. Silber was subsequently hired on at Boston University, where he eventually became president of the university. I wonder whether he found any qualified black professors to hire there.

» *A Kerfuffle over the Bar Exam*

In retrospect, it might've made more sense to pursue a PhD in political science. I enjoyed poli-sci more than law, and as a result I didn't take law school that seriously. I kind of skated by, not bothering to specialize in a branch of law or worry about my grades. I worried more about my students' grades at Huston-Tillotson. It probably surprised no one when, upon graduation from UT, I took the bar exam but accepted a full-time teaching position at Huston-Tillotson instead, eventually becoming the head of the government department.

My experience with the bar exam is its own funny story. At the time it was mortifying, but forty-five years later I can laugh about it. In brief, I was arrested for driving while intoxicated, but the charges were later dropped (and rightfully so). What happened was that my deeply rooted self-doubts about my ability to succeed as a lawyer were further magnified by well-meaning friends in Austin. They told me I'd never graduate from UT, as they didn't know any other black who had. I graduated all right, but then those same people started saying I'd never pass the bar exam. Of all the blacks to graduate law school in the entire state of Texas, only a few had ever passed the bar and gone into practice. You can understand why I was so nervous!

I decided to take an extra one-night course to study specifically for the bar. Pat drove me to the class and then picked me up afterward. After completing that course, I was still too nervous to take the bar exam, so I decided to take the course a second time. Pat refused to take me to the class the second time or to pick me up afterward. He said that I would have to drive myself there and back. So, I took the new, still-rather-shiny Thunderbird downtown, parked it on Congress, and entered the hotel in which the class was being held.

Two other blacks were taking the course that night. It was being offered by a man named Mitchell, a Bastrop lawyer and all-around nice guy. I thought the course went well. To celebrate the end of the course, Mitchell offered me a shot of bad scotch. I took just one swallow before I knew that cheap liquor would make me sick, so I excused myself back outside to my car. Two police officers watched me exit the building, get in my Thunderbird, roll down the window, and proceed to throw up!

To this day, I wonder if maybe they didn't think I was a prostitute, coming out of a hotel and getting into a fancy car. At any rate, they arrested me for a DWI. I told them I wasn't drunk, just sick, but all the crying probably didn't help. If they had breathalyzer tests then, they never gave me one. Rather than keep me overnight in jail, Judge Ronnie Earle allowed Pat to take me home. A few weeks later, having hired Frank Maloney (the best lawyer in town!), I defended myself before a jury in the county court.

Prior to the trial, my lawyer warned me not to bring Pat inside the courtroom. "Blacks don't hardly show up for jury duty," he counseled me, "so you're gonna be faced with a white jury. It's best you don't bring your husband to court, because he looks too white and the jury won't take well to a mixed marriage." Heeding his advice, we won the case, and I walked away without so much as probation or community service. Afterward, I asked my lawyer if I should have the charges expunged. "No need," he said. "You were found not guilty." Thus, I left that day a free woman and, later, a licensed lawyer.

» *Huston-Tillotson Gets a Pre-Law Society*

Several really significant events occurred over the five years (1969–1974) I headed Huston-Tillotson's government department.

First, I organized a pre-law society. Huston-Tillotson graduates going on to become lawyers were originally few and far between, but that pre-law society started converting them in droves. The guaranteed scholarships I secured for society members to attend a pre-law conference each summer were part of the draw. Maybe you've heard of the Fleming twins, who are outstanding lawyers today, or Stan Kerr, the ad hoc judge and attorney for the mentally ill in the probate court. They all came through Huston-Tillotson. Only Stan Kerr, Francharm Gibson, and a couple of others went on to UT for law school. I don't blame those who didn't, because the UT minority-admissions recruiter during those years was a man by the name of Professor Green, who kept denying admission to black H-T applicants to UT's law school. He didn't really believe black students could be successful. I wrote a letter of complaint to Judge Garwood, who sat on the board at H-T and was on the fifth circuit, and he mediated a discussion between Green and me. It must've borne some fruit, because a few H-T students were accepted at UT after that, including Stan Kerr (who had attended H-T even though he was white).

Relations between Huston-Tillotson and UT were not healed overnight. When a UT political scientist approached me about partnering students from the government departments of UT and H-T, the head of his department, Dr. Livingston (who was not a patron of integration at UT), instantly put the kibosh on our plans. Dr. Livingston was somewhat revered in Austin, and his sentiments influenced UT for longer than I would have liked. That young political scientist soon left UT for the University of Virginia. Today, UT has come so far. UT's Division of Diversity and Community Engagement now works with black and Hispanic students from H-T to help them prepare for law school.

» *Examining Apartheid in South Africa*

The second significant event was my appointment by David Newson, the Assistant Secretary of State for African Affairs, to the US State Department's advisory council of the Bureau of African Affairs in 1970. I'd drawn a lot of attention that year for the work I was doing to improve the quality of African American life, and The Struggle equally embraced our brothers and sisters in the homeland. The advisory council met twice a year at the State Department, or four times total over my two-year appointment. It was the first time I sat on a committee that exclusively used round tables, à la King Arthur and the Knights of the Round Table—the idea being that no one held a place of more importance than anyone else. Without a head or a tail, all committee members, black or white, were inherently equal, and we carried that message with us on our data-finding commission to South Africa in 1971. It soon became obvious, though, that South Africa didn't share our perspective.

From 1948 to 1994, South Africa practiced a system of racial segregation not altogether unlike that which once divided America. Instead of Jim Crow, it was called apartheid, and apartheid recognized three categories of South Africans: black Africans, coloreds, and whites. The term *coloreds* here refers to the descendants of unions between Dutch settlers and African women as well as to the occasional Asian immigrant. The system seems straightforward enough, but within a single generation's time, continued interbreeding made it difficult to always tell the races apart. White government officials therefore devised the comb test, meant to reclassify otherwise unclassifiable individuals. Should a comb run straight through a given man's hair, the man probably had some white in him; should the comb get stuck, he was African, because Africans had nappy hair. By mutual agreement, the coloreds separated themselves from the Africans, and the whites separated themselves from both the coloreds and the Africans. In this way, apartheid produced a very complicated society.

Seeing as our own council was rather mixed, we weren't sure how we'd be received in South Africa. Among our numbers were Ned Munger, a white professor of geography from Caltech; a black minister; a young, white graduate student; and me (the only female). Our job was to collect data about apartheid and report back to the US State Department. The council's findings may have been influential later in convincing the US Congress to pass the Mandela Freedom Resolution, which freed beloved South African activist Nelson Mandela from a term of life imprisonment. For the most part, I think we all felt safe. We were VIP visitors. Nobody questioned us if we went someplace only whites were allowed. We had no problems with the restaurants.

In 1971, the US ambassador to South Africa was a man from Texas named John Hurd. A white Republican, he'd probably never in his life socialized with black people, but he at least put on a good show of believing in diversity. Ambassador Hurd threw a state dinner for us, to which he even invited a few Africans. I was seated next to one of them—a colored woman who could not contain her excitement. She came from a town where discrimination was strong, and she could not believe she'd been invited to the Cape Town embassy. When the black limousine had arrived to pick her up, her town's whole populace had turned out to watch.

Traveling from conference to conference around the country, we had plenty of opportunity to witness discrimination firsthand. We visited many US-owned local businesses, from car dealerships to factories, and noted the often unsafe or unfair working conditions. Arriving at one factory during lunchtime, we inquired about the weak bowls of mealie-meal being served to black workers. We were told, "Oh, the Africans love it!" Really, though, it was just the cheapest food they could serve to all those people. We learned how white South African men often crossed the border to Swaziland, an all-black country, because casinos were legal there. Most of them kept black or colored South African or Swaziland mistresses, or they had whole second families in that country.

One of our early stops was the Transkei, a "republic" set aside for

Xhosa-speaking people (Xhosa being a Bantu, or click-consonant, language). You can think of it as the equivalent of a Native American reservation. Mandela was from the Transkei. We did all meet with the Transkei's black longtime governor, Kaiser Mantanzima, but everything else was entirely segregated. Whites couldn't go anywhere that had been deemed "black," including a black bar that the reverend and I could patronize but the white members of our party could not.

Despite a vast crevasse of cultural differences, Kaiser Mantanzima and I hit it off right away. On a lark, I invited the governor and his wife to visit Austin sometime. They'd seen the giant longhorn steer that John Hurd, a fellow Texan, had sent to South Africa's president, and they were eager to see a country of such abundance. I had no idea they'd actually come, but soon enough Pat and I were helping Governor and Mrs. Mantanzima check into an Austin hotel and chauffeuring them around to take in the sights and sounds. One morning we even drove to Prairie View A&M. As the highways weren't much built up then, there were cows everywhere. Kaiser said Texas reminded him exactly of home.

We tried to make the Mantanzimas feel just as much like the guests of honor as I had in South Africa. The president of Prairie View hosted a reception for them, but I wanted to go even bigger. In one of the Austin papers, I read how the state of Texas had spent $600,000 in taxpayer dollars to renovate the home of the UT chancellor. He and his family lived in the house in Tarrytown (a wealthy Austin neighborhood). I got to thinking that if I, as a taxpayer, had in part funded those renovations, I ought to be entitled to using the property. Right away I called the chancellor himself, Dr. William Cunningham, and asked if I might organize a reception for the Transkei governor and his wife there. Dr. Cunningham agreed at once; I guess no other black had had the nerve to even approach the idea. Together we compiled a list of all the prominent blacks and whites in the community, and we ended up throwing a very successful affair. Kaiser Mantanzima was so impressed. I still see Dr. Cunningham at football games!

» On Blood Diamonds

Because of my trip to South Africa with the Bureau of African Affairs, I was invited to a conference the following year outside Louisville, Kentucky, at which the keynote speaker was to be the present owner of the De Beers Mine, the largest exporter of South African diamonds. "Blood diamonds" as a concept still existed in the abstract then; the speaker was therefore hailed as a business magnate rather than condemned as a murderer. I'd been to the Transkei, though, and I'd seen the disparity in the flesh. I've no doubt that man gave money to all the charities he listed, but his Louisville admirers didn't realize that it was at the expense of the African miners. They hadn't watched broken women sweep the dirt floors of ramshackle huts, choking on the continual smoke from cooking fires and waiting on their husbands to send money that never arrived back from the mines they had been drafted to work in. It was one of the most horrible situations I've ever witnessed. Seeing those women had made me cry and wonder how people could even live under such conditions, yet the atmosphere at the conference was celebratory.

It makes me sad to admit, but I, too, had cause to celebrate in Kentucky. John Deere was the conference sponsor, since they'd manufactured most of the equipment being used in the mines, and the government had paid my entire way to and from Louisville. It was a personal honor that also reflected well on Huston-Tillotson University, where I was head of the government department, and it afforded me the opportunity to reconnect with an old friend in Kentucky and visit the racetrack. I guess all of us were hypocrites that weekend. (And I don't say that lightly.)

» *Foreign Reaction to the Montgomery Bus Boycott*

The fourth significant event to happen while I was teaching at Huston-Tillotson was my application for and receipt of a prestigious research grant that took me to Montgomery, Alabama, in 1972. The year 1975 would mark the twenty-year anniversary of the beginning of the Montgomery bus boycott, and to solemnize the occasion I'd decided to undertake a public project. The Montgomery bus boycott started when Rosa Parks, an African American woman, refused to give up her bus seat to a white person—an act of social protest for which she was arrested and that touched off a year-long boycott of the bus system by Montgomery's black populace. Under MLK Jr.'s leadership, the boycott dealt a serious blow to Montgomery's economy. Even when white agitators firebombed King's house in response, he continued to preach nonviolent protest. His eventual arrest earned the boycott international attention and likely put pressure on the 1956 case of *Browder v. Gayle*, the decision in which segregated buses were ultimately declared unconstitutional.

The project I'd won funding for proposed an investigation into and analysis of the countless letters that M. L. had received from leaders around the world during the boycott. On my arrival in Alabama, I combed through whole file cabinets of letters. While a few of them criticized or even threatened the reverend, the overwhelming majority saluted his actions, sending love and support from the farthest regions of the world. It seemed natural to assume, and M. L. confirmed, that such an outpouring of foreign support greatly encouraged him and contributed to his not standing down but boldly defying an illogical justice system that punished seemingly at whim. I ended up writing an article that detailed the international reaction to the Montgomery bus boycott, and I published it through one of the

HBCUs in South Carolina. I don't include it here, however, because they didn't edit the piece; they published my article complete with every editorial mistake. I'm still so embarrassed that if you want to read it, you'll have to look it up yourself!

» *Travel to Gratz, Austria*

Finally, the fifth significant event in as many years was my winning a fellowship to study abroad in Gratz, Austria. A whole group of us went to document the sociopolitical climate of Eastern Europe, including Austria, Czechoslovakia, and Poland. In Poland, we visited Auschwitz—and we're talking not but twenty-five years or so after the end of World War II. The camps felt haunted, and the "museum" that Poland had turned them into was very revealing. From Nazi gas chambers to lobby cases displaying collections of eyeglasses and shorn hair, our tour affected me deeply and reminded me of something M. L. once said: "Injustice anywhere is a threat to justice everywhere."

I had actually first developed empathy for the Jewish plight during my research into Israel for my master's thesis. Learning about the work of Jewish leaders, given their own history of slavery in Egypt, to help end African slavery only increased my fondness for the Jewish people and made Auschwitz that much more of a personal experience. Anyone who helps the black cause is all right in my book!

Among my European travel companions was Dr. Terry Brookens, who was by then a professor but whom I'd first met while I was in law school at UT and he was a PhD candidate. Terry and I used to get lunch together at Simkins Hall* on campus, and you could say that, perhaps like an older brother, he took me under his wing. "Harriet," he told me one day when we were students, "there are two things I would not like for the white people on campus to see you doing." He

---

*In 2010, President Powers requested that the Texas Board of Regents change the name of Simkins Residence Hall (named after a UT professor of law prominent in the Ku Klux Klan in the 1800s) to Creekside Residence Hall. The Board voted unanimously to implement the change.

said, "Don't ever let them see you eating watermelon when we go for lunch, and don't ever let them see you sleeping in the library." The watermelon thing was a reference to the stereotype that all southern blacks loved watermelon; some of the mansions in which whites lived even had lawn statues made that depicted black boys eating watermelon by the mansion gates. I think the sleeping-in-the-library remark had to do with the stereotype that blacks were lazy. Like I was, Terry was acutely aware of UT's racist past, and he wanted no part in contributing to stereotypes or lending them any more validity. I told Terry I'd try my hardest to stay awake in the library, although we didn't have computers then, just huge, heavy books to lift and read. "But I'm not gonna let anybody ever stop me from eating watermelon!" I said. And that was that.

» *Harriet Murphy, JD*

In all my years, I never did practice law full time. Instead, I maintained a small, solo practice on the side while devoting most of my energy to teaching. At least a couple of stories from my years practicing law stand out in my memory, however, so I'll relate them in the next few pages.

To preface, you should know that I really wasn't into civil-liability law. I tended to handle divorces, small criminal cases, and the like. So, when a concerned individual contacted me about a possible graveyard violation by none other than AT&T, everyone's favorite telecommunications conglomerate, I was rather out of my league. If you're thinking, *A sole practitioner took on a giant company in a field she wasn't even that experienced in? What the #%&!*?*, then you've probably grasped the fact that I stood absolutely no chance and should have made a complete and total fool of myself, in every sense of the word. But here's what actually happened.

There used to be (and may still be today) a white Baptist church off Braker Lane in North Austin. During Reconstruction, the church allowed blacks to attend, but they had to sit in a separate, roped-off section. Growing simultaneously more tired of segregation and richer as free people with every passing day, the blacks soon built their own church not too far down the road. On the church grounds, they built a cemetery, and next to that church they built a foster home. Fast forward a century: the church building had been moved across I-35, but the cemetery, of course, remained in its original spot. As it turned out, AT&T needed to run some underground wires through the graveyard, and they'd erroneously (although understandably) sought permission from the white Baptist church up the road. What no one understands is how and why the pastor at the white church granted AT&T a permit to enter the land that his church didn't even own.

By the time I got involved, AT&T had already laid the wires. A black descendant of someone buried in the cemetery had pressed charges on the grounds that AT&T might disturb his ancestor's gravesite. To me, that seemed a really serious offense, permit or no. AT&T's defense was that in laying the wires, they'd restored the previously neglected cemetery to a much nicer state, clearing lots of brush and debris in addition to covering their own tracks. Certainly, that had been an act of kindness—but disturbing graves? Could brush clearing recompense that kind of violation in any real way?

After agreeing to represent the individual, my first task was to organize a company. I gathered that man and several of his black relatives and formed a legal corporation. AT&T, meanwhile, sent their lawyer over to try to scare me off the case. He showed up at my office at Huston-Tillotson saying, "You know what, Mrs. Murphy? I'm gonna flood you with so many papers that you'll never be able to respond to them, discoveries and all." His threats worked; I was frightened to death. Rather than back down, however, I hired another black lawyer to help me. I also secured the help of one of my former students at Huston-Tillotson, Stan Kerr, to research the history of the cemetery. When we had our ducks in a row, we went to the press.

Nothing gets the public riled up like corporate giants taking advantage of innocent civilians. Just as soon as I broke the story about AT&T tearing up a graveyard without the permission of the people whose relatives were buried there, AT&T changed their tune. They told me I'd had no right to go public with the case—although I absolutely did—and to get out of the spotlight as quickly as possible, they offered to settle out of court. I was so happy not only to have won in the face of impossible odds but also to be able to compensate the family. A trust was formed to maintain the graveyard from that point on. Today, there's a fence around the property.

» *Why Black Lawyers Had It Harder*

The only other two cases worth relating highlight just how unhealthy the environment of Austin was for African American lawyers practicing in the 1960s and 1970s. There was another reason I didn't practice full time that had nothing to do with teaching at H-T, and that was the fact that practicing law simply was not lucrative for blacks. Big law firms were not receptive to hiring black lawyers, and very few legal positions existed at the state government level. Solo practice was the only option left, but you could hardly get retained when even blacks believed that they were better represented by white lawyers who they thought wielded more influence in the courtroom.

I remember on multiple occasions walking into the probation office to pick up paperwork for my clients and being scolded for not waiting for my lawyer, as though I was the defendant. The only thing to do was to bear it with a smile—until I realized you can use people's prejudices and other preconceived notions against them. For example, at my first jury trial in the municipal court, I had the nerve to defend a client on a public intoxication charge who already had a record of public intoxication. I believed my client was arrested primarily because he was black and secondarily for urinating on the side of the street. He admitted to having only one beer that night. When the jury found him not guilty, both Judge Ronnie Earle and I were stunned. In talking to some of the jurors after the trial, I learned that the forewoman (and the only black on the jury) had delivered the verdict more or less single-handedly by confirming what the white jurors wanted to hear: that African Americans were ignorant, helpless, and so on. The defendant was uneducated, she reminded them, and therefore unaware of the public accommodation law of 1964. He didn't know he could relieve himself at a gas station; he did what he had to do during the days of segregation, and it didn't mean he was drunk.

On another case—and this was in probate court, which I started to do a little more of after the AT&T debacle—I represented a black family before an all-white jury purposely chosen for the occasion. The case involved a will contest, wherein my clients had inherited several acres of prime land in South Austin despite being only caregivers of (rather than related to) the deceased. The deceased's relatives were, of course, contesting. I knew how strongly blacks believed in the notion that "blood is thicker than water"; a black jury would have given the land to the family. Instead, my white partner and I won with a white jury that valued the caregivers' service.

PART III » MAJOR POLITICAL CONTRIBUTIONS

Black America still wears chains.
—MARTIN LUTHER KING JR.,
from an essay titled "The Negro and the Constitution"
in the 1944 yearbook of Booker T. Washington High School,
Atlanta, Georgia

» *Carter for the Win*

In 1976, I broke my ankle, was elected as a presidential elector, and took the oaths of a full-time judge—all in that order.

The ankle I broke by running down a grassy bank and falling, an accident so bad it landed me in the hospital. In a complete fan-girl moment, I had been running after the black professional golfer Charlie Sifford, who was playing in Austin that day, when I snapped a couple of tendons, requiring surgery.

I only remember the year because it was from that hospital gurney that I received two important phone calls on the beige, plastic bedside telephone: one informing me about the electorship and one about my judgeship.

First, the electorship.

According to the Constitution of the United States, US presidents are to be elected by presidential electors, who are themselves elected from the various states of the union. The number of electors (and electoral votes) in each state is equal to the number of members of Congress to which that state is entitled. Electoral votes are cast according to the popular vote. The candidate receiving the highest number of electoral votes becomes president. Seems pretty straightforward, no?

Things get weird, though, when you learn that electoral votes sometimes but do not always coincide with the popular vote. Whichever candidate wins the popular vote in Texas, for example, receives the electoral votes for Texas (of which there are currently thirty-eight); because we don't directly add the popular votes a candidate wins in one state to the votes he or she wins in another state, however, a candidate can become president even without having a majority of the nation's popular vote. In other words, a Republican who wins all the traditionally red states receives the electoral votes for those states, and if the total number of electoral votes for the Republican party from the

President Jimmy Carter and me, after I served as a Democratic presidential elector for the state.

swing states is greater than the total number of electoral votes for the Democratic party, *independent of* the actual tallied numbers of popular votes, then the Republican candidate wins.

It's happened five times that a candidate won the presidency without winning the popular vote: John Quincy Adams, Rutherford B. Hayes, Benjamin Harrison, George W. Bush in 2000, and Donald Trump in 2016.

On the Monday following the popular vote, the state electors meet at the Capitol to cast the electoral votes. Each elector casts his or her vote in accordance with how the state voted, and that's it. Casting your ballot comes at the end of a whole year's work leading up to the election, though. I was elected as a Carter delegate to the state convention, and I helped out his campaign. When Jimmy Carter won the presidency in November 1976, I was and remain to this day the only

African American woman to serve as a Democratic presidential elector for the state of Texas.

Afterward, all the electors are invited to the president's inauguration in Washington, DC. The red carpet is rolled out, and they get VIP seating at the ceremony. Pat went with me to President Carter's inauguration, and we were seated immediately behind Senator John Warner of Virginia and his wife, Elizabeth Taylor. Taylor had a fur hat on and just looked gorgeous.

» *Murphy's Law*

I'd been a part-time judge for three years when I received a full-time appointment in 1976. Becoming a full-time judge meant leaving Huston-Tillotson for good (although I later returned in a reduced capacity) and also forgoing further practice as a lawyer. It meant joining a multitude of committees for social and political change, planning all kinds of events, and even introducing legislation. Most of all, as the first African American woman to be appointed a judge in Texas, it meant confronting racial backbite in the courts head-on, given that the judicial system has always (and ironically so) favored nepotism over honorable merit. I faced so much opposition from the white associate judges that I used to say I dodged more political bullets from critics than American soldiers in Afghanistan dodged real bullets.

For fifteen years, I served as an associate judge in Austin's municipal court, helping the public to fight its battles while more quietly waging my own war. In 1988, I became presiding judge, a role I filled for five years more—meaning my appointments spanned more than two decades all told. The real trouble began with my presiding judgeship, which seemed to make me more enemies (and powerful ones at that) than admirers.

Although the newspapers reported that I "competed" with other judges for the position, it's not like we were campaigning for the popular vote. Presiding judges are nominated by the mayor and appointed via a majority vote of the city council. All the brown-nosing is therefore internal: picture the typical scenario in which politicians form alliances and trade favors. I was never much interested in that scene until the day I didn't have a choice. Shortly after my appointment was announced, one female judge (who shall remain nameless) approached me in the hallway to say that she should have been presiding judge. "The only reason you got the job," she sneered, "is because

Judge Harriet M. Murphy

you're black." I'd known she hated me, but I didn't know in that moment how to respond. Fueled later by a litany of perfect comebacks, I settled (in my head) on: "Too bad for you that you aren't black, then!" I never did say it to her face.

Sometime after that, a motion was proposed to grant the presiding judge more administrative power. That female judge made it her

> GEORGIA ASSOCIATION OF EDUCATORS
>
> 3951 Snapfinger Parkway
> Decatur, Georgia 30035
>
> April 4, 1978
>
> Mrs. Harritee M. Murphy
> Judge, Municipal Court
> Austin, Texas
>
> Dear Miss Mitchell:
>
> The Atlanta Daily World has been informative to keep your students, friends and associates aware of your frequent visits to Atlanta and some of your contributions made to the state of Texas.
>
> Every time I hear of you, being one of my favorite teachers so many years ago at South Fulton, naturally, I have to relive the pass with your many memories you instilled which are dear to the heart even today.
>
> My first surprise was to learn that you had married. Secondly, you had become a lawyer and doing private practice and teaching at Huston-Tillotson College, and now the big one: J U D G E.
>
> I am reminded of my Grandmother's expression, "Good Things Come To Good Peoples!" and what is happening with you is very indicative to this fact. (When you send me your picture, I shall see if she will remember your racing me home on one of your family visitation days without telling me you were visiting and not bringing the bad news and walked the distance in your highest heels and kept a smile on your beaming face.)
>
> Let me assure you that my life was affected by your passing my way and I shall never forget you for the memories still stand out as if it was yesterday than years.
>
> With every good wish for your continued success and happiness, I am
>
> Respectfully yours,
>
> Raymon A. King, II.
>
> rak

It was wonderful to be remembered fondly by one of my South Fulton High School students years later.

personal mission to stop the motion in its tracks, and she lobbied to bring as many people in power to her side as possible. To this day, I can't say for sure whether it was her or someone else who leaked damaging stories about me to the press—about cases that had been handled in perfect accordance with the law but called my character into question all the same. There were misleading headlines about how I personally had Class C criminals jailed on warrants when the legal recourse was but a fine, and the accompanying stories failed to mention how those same criminals were only jailed after failing to pay the warrant fees (a system I later did away with entirely). She and her co-

conspirators were trying to make me look bad while boosting their own images in the public eye. It was simply too bad for her that she left a paper trail of her plots.

One day I was again walking down the hallway when a secretary approached me. It must have taken some nerve, because she slipped me a copy she'd made of a letter she'd found that was addressed from the female judge to another white judge. In brief, the letter was practically a written confession of conspiracy. Phrases like "move [Harriet] along" clearly alluded to removing me from office. The other judges must not have realized I had so many friends, especially among the "little people" like that brave, kind secretary, or they surely would've been more careful.

The first action I took was to hire an expert to come to the court and test all the typewriters in the building to confirm whose typewriter the note had come from. This man met me at the building at 10:00 p.m. and verified that the female judge's typewriter matched the evidence. Armed finally with concrete proof, it was time to call in my own favors.

I knew the white judges were in cahoots with a prominent presiding judge from Dallas, because I'd seen them whispering together in an office. The day after receiving the secretary's letter, I took it up to the Texas Legislature, found a black legislator I knew from Dallas, and told him what was going on. He assured me he'd intervene with the out-of-line Dallas judge, but it was too little, too late. The council vote was the next day, and by the time all the judge's friends had finished testifying against me, the council did not approve any changes to my existing administrative powers.

In the end, none of it really mattered. Those white judges found themselves exposed for who they really were, and not a one was reappointed. Deeply tired of what had been a constant battle for me (one that was worth it, certainly, but a hard one all the same), I decided to retire rather than return to the bench for reappointment. By then it was 1993, and I know the black judge who preceded me faced very few, if any, of the challenges that I had. Times were changing, and all I could say is that it was about time!

» *Accomplishments from the Bench*

What follows is a quick review of my more notable accomplishments as presiding judge of the Austin municipal court—because I believe in leaving a place better than I found it.

I combed through Austin's pool of black lawyers to handpick those who would become Austin's second and third (after me) black associate judges. One of them was Evelyn McKee, who later also became the presiding judge. Another was Sandra Fitzpatrick, a municipal court judge in Round Rock.

As chair of the Greater Austin Council on Alcoholism and Drug Abuse and chair of the city's first detoxification task force, I helped organize a rehabilitation program that got addicts off the street and back into the workforce. I received a distinguished service award in 1990 for the amount of time and money saved by the municipal court, which had to process fewer and fewer repeat offenders as a result of the program. Applying the same model to the Task Force for the Homeless, we put people into shelters and reduced the number of panhandling cases (begging was illegal in Austin in the 1970s and 1980s) and other petty crimes, positively impacting a system too often glutted by the same weary faces.

To further reduce the number of defendants whose main "crime" was poverty, I instituted a partial-payment plan by which poor people, rather than being arrested, could make incremental deposits toward their tickets or other owed fines. The main problem with the original design was that it took Class C crimes (normally punishable only by fines) and made them jailable offenses when warrants were issued for noncompliance to pay. Tell me how it makes sense to go to the expense of jailing someone overnight just because they couldn't afford fifty dollars all at once? Nonsense. Partial-payment plans kept incarceration rates down and even zeroed out tickets owed in the long run, such that today partial payments are the norm. The plans weren't available in Travis County in the 1970s and 1980s, though—I was the first to establish the system in Austin!

To keep track of all these overhauls, I drafted and lobbied a bill formally making Austin's municipal court a court of record. That just means there's a court clerk present who records court proceedings and makes them available as evidence of fact. Before my bill, Austin's municipal court was a court not of record, in which a judge rules based on notes and memory. Any time a person loses a case in a court not of record, he or she can take that same case to a county court on a form of appeal called a *trial de novo* and have the case heard again as though no prior trial had been held. You'd think courts of record would be the standard everywhere, but they weren't in Travis County in the 1980s.

Finally, I established an environmental court in Austin to oversee the proper permitting of restaurants and other public facilities. The environmental court (today called the community court) tries violations of the health code, for example, and similar city regulations in the best interests of the public.

» *Here Come the Judges*

Sometime in the mid-1980s, I participated in Spelman's SASE (Spelman Alumna Student Externship) program. Started by Barbara Anthony Brown, associate director of institutional effectiveness, the point of the program was to introduce young Spelman women to nontraditional career paths—including law. Each year during Spelman's spring break, SASE sent current students all over the country to live with established Spelman graduates and learn about fields they might like to pursue. I hosted several such students over two or three years who had dreams of going to law school. One student I recall with particular fondness was Natalie Frazier. She went on to law school at George Washington University and coincidentally married Hugh Allen, the son of my friend Eleanor Allen. Naturally, I took the students to visit UT's School of Law and the law fraternity as well as a few of the law offices around Austin. Any time there was an event that was sponsored by lawyers, we would attend, and of course there was always a visit to the courts to meet the judges. One year a fellow lawyer even took the students on a boat ride down Town Lake. Spelman students lined up to come to Austin after hearing about the students' time with me!

Spelman College then contacted me in the early 1990s about a student from Austin named Laralen Houston who was one credit hour short of graduating. They asked whether I would oversee her independent study so that she might graduate on time. Due, I suppose, to her interest in politics, the student decided to focus her study on *me*. Part of her self-designed course work included making a scrapbook called *Here Come the Judges* that chronicles my years as a municipal court judge. It's thanks to her that I have copies of nearly every newspaper article to mention my name over twenty years, plus photos and

I loved being a judge, including the contact with Austin residents and the feeling of satisfaction I got from helping people. I was named Presiding Municipal Court Judge in 1988.

award certificates. A lot of old memories surface when I look back at their headlines and captions.

- "Fake Hotel Worker Stabs Woman 9 Times." I set bail on that case.
- "Slaying God's Will." That was a chilling case about the mother of an eighteen-year-old strangled by her uncle. Mom did nothing to stop the attack because she thought it was God's will that her daughter die. I set bail on it too.
- "Municipal Judges' Docket Lacking in Drama." This headline seems ironic after the previous two, but we really didn't deal in a lot of drama, because a municipal judge is the first judge that a person arrested by the Austin police sees.*

When all is said and done, I really loved judging. I loved the work, the contact with the people, and the feeling of satisfaction I got from helping people. Being a judge is like being a social worker and a psychologist all at the same time—and the mediocre salary is somewhere between the two!

---

*Municipal judges warn defendants of their rights, make sure that police have probable cause to charge someone with a crime, and set bail. They don't conduct higher criminal trials, only Class C cases. In other words, the municipal courts have jurisdiction over criminal misdemeanors punishable by fine only (no confinement), municipal ordinance criminal cases, and magistrate functions, along with city code violations.

» "Retirement"

Like I could ever actually retire! As soon as I stepped down from the presiding judgeship I started to get bored. At sixty-six years old, I went right back to practicing part-time law and teaching a class or two at Huston-Tillotson.

In the 1990s, race relations had in some ways much improved in America. There was greater general public access and more opportunities for African Americans. But 1992 became immortalized as the tipping point for police brutality against minorities. The beating of Rodney King, a black taxi driver, by four LAPD officers and the subsequent acquittal of three of those four officers sparked a nationwide series of violent riots that left fifty-three dead and over two thousand injured before the National Guard intervened. The Ferguson, Missouri, unrest in 2014 was like LA all over again, what with the looting and burning—only in that case, the victim, Michael Brown, died. There have since been far too many unnecessary minority deaths at the hands of police.

That type of blind, unthinking violence is exactly what a Hispanic professor, Dr. Mary E. DeFerreire, and I attempted to address and quash with our jointly taught course, Can We All Get Along? When Rodney King gave his first statement following his recovery, such was the question he posed to the world, and a very good one it was. Can We All Get Along? combined African American and Hispanic politics at H-T. The dream was not just to teach two subjects but also to bring black and Hispanic students together in the classroom. At the end of the semester, we opened up the programming to facilitate an all-campus conference on the topic. Both class and conference were so successful that Robert Berdahl, president of UT from 1993 to 1997, invited Dr. DeFerreire and I to bring our program material to his office to review the possibility of creating such a class for UT. UT officials wanted to review it for the possibility of offering at UT too. Unfortunately, extenuating circumstances prevented us from doing so.

» *Vacation Time!*

With slightly more free time on my hands, I started attending the annual midwinter conference of the National Bar Association's Judicial Council. It's always held on some tropical island, where we can enjoy the island culture as well as the weather. Barbados, Jamaica, and St. Martin are three of the islands that I have visited through the NBAJC. On each, we were entertained by the island's attorneys and other government officials and allowed plenty of free time to explore the casinos and the beach.

As often as Pat was able, he accompanied me on these trips. Since we never did have a honeymoon, I loved getting to travel with my husband, who got handsomer by the day. The only trip he couldn't make was the St. Martin conference, as he'd lost his passport and we couldn't find it anywhere. He showed up at the airport anyway, hoping he could squeak through with his driver's license, but security personnel demanded Pat's birth certificate at a minimum. As Pat was born in Arkansas, it was too much trouble to get a copy at that late hour, so I went ahead without him.

Just a few years ago, I had the opportunity to go to Cancun. Pat had already passed by this time, so I invited my dear friend Doris Hall. "Let's go sit on the beach and talk about all our old boyfriends," I said, but Doris's mom was ailing in a nursing home, and Doris didn't feel like she could leave her. It's just as well, because she and I have outlived all those men anyway. Arnold Cameron, my first boyfriend at Morehouse, has since died, as have the two or three Tuskegee cadets I dated after him. Only Joel Balkans, a dentist friend in Houston with whom I had one or two dates, is still kicking. Not too long ago, he said, "I'm lucky, Harriet, that you and I never became a couple, as all your other boyfriends are dead now!"

That's why it's highly advisable, ladies, to make good girlfriends and hold them close. You never know when you'll want to have a margarita and a laugh on the beach!

» The O. J. Simpson Trial

If you don't know about the O. J. Simpson trial, you were probably living under a rock in 1995. Just in case, however, I'll give you a bit of the background. Basically, O. J. Simpson was a former professional athlete who was accused in 1994 of murdering his ex-wife, Nicole Brown Simpson, and a waiter, Ronald Goldman, in Los Angeles. Brown and Goldman were found brutally stabbed to death outside Brown's apartment. The story was that Nicole's mother had left her glasses at the restaurant at which Ronald was a waiter, and he had stopped by Brown's place to drop them off, unintentionally arriving just as Brown's assailant was killing her. At the same time, police found lit candles around Nicole's bathtub, as though she'd been expecting someone—possibly Ronald. O. J.'s motives were given as jealousy and a way to get out from under the several thousands of dollars a month he had to pay Nicole in child support for their two kids.

Complicating the case were all kinds of contradictory reports, including eyewitness accounts that placed Simpson at the scene and Simpson's own testimony that he spent the night packing for a conference in Chicago. There was also evidence that no one could really make heads or tails of: a single bloody glove, bloody socks, bloody shoe prints, and blood in Simpson's Bronco. All of it seemed to incriminate Simpson but at the same time appeared to have been planted. A suspicious cut on O. J.'s hand was said to have resulted from an accident. The trial lasted more than nine months and was televised daily to an enormous viewership, prompting *People of the State of California v. Orenthal James Simpson* to be dubbed The Trial of the Century.

Probably the trial drew so much national attention because Simpson had been a football player, because the murder was so graphic and the case so dramatic, because Nicole was white and O. J. was black, and because Simpson hired a rather high-profile defense team. Regardless, the public was riveted, and Austin was no exception—and that's where I entered the picture. In keeping with every other major publication across the country, the *Austin American-Statesman* newspaper decided to formulate its own daily analysis of the ongoing proceedings. The editors invited four very different Austinites to watch the trial each day and give their opinions on that day's events; the goal was not to pronounce a verdict necessarily but to comment on court procedure and the various characters in the drama, reporting the introduction of new testimonies and the constant resultant shifts in public opinion.

I was chosen, or so the *Statesman* editor told me, because I was "well known for speaking my mind and saying whatever I thought about whatever I was confronted with." Assigned to be "Trial Watchers" with me were a thirty-seven-year-old white female auditor, a nineteen-year-old white male student, and a thirty-two-year-old white female homemaker. From the opening statements on January 24, 1995, to the not-guilty verdict on October 3 of that year, we duly reported daily. It was terribly exciting and, I felt, a great honor to participate. Whether calling out the prosecutor, who had a knack for swinging Judge Ito around to his side, or sharing the story of the seventy-one-year-old African American female juror who said she could relate to O. J.'s mother and was herself a victim of police brutality during the civil rights movement, it was actually *fun* to just spout off every day and know that everyone in Austin was reading what I wrote.

Do I think O. J. is guilty? As a retired lawyer and judge, I know that's not really the question. The question is whether the state proved its case beyond a reasonable doubt, and no, I don't think it did. Thus, I agree with the not-guilty verdict, even if I personally harbor some doubts. I also don't think the makeup of the jury had anything to do with the trial outcome. The fact that nine of twelve jurors were black led many spectators to insist that O. J. got off because he was black too. Prosecutor Marcia Clark sharply criticized the jurors, telling CNN that "a majority black jury won't bring justice." Everyone forgot, I guess, about the case of former Chicago congressman Mel

Reynolds, unanimously convicted by black jurors that same year on charges of criminal sexual abuse, child pornography, and obstruction of justice for having sex with a sixteen-year-old. I'm black, but my opinions have nothing to do with the color of Simpson's skin; I feel only that the state didn't prove his guilt.

Although Simpson was acquitted in the criminal trial, he later lost a civil suit pressed by Brown's and Goldman's families over the same issue: the unlawful death of two people. Whereas to win a criminal case, the prosecution must prove a defendant to be guilty beyond reasonable doubt, to win a civil case requires merely a preponderance of evidence: that is, having more evidence than the other side. Civil suits don't result in jail time but in fines of restitution; if you can't pay, they go for collateral: your physical and intellectual property. In February 1997, Simpson was ordered to pay damages of $40 million to the Brown and Goldman families, a judgment upheld the next year on appeal.

O. J. Simpson was sentenced to a 33-year prison term for unrelated felonies, including armed robbery and kidnapping. He was released on parole after ten years, in 2017.

» *Abigail Fisher and the Top 10 Percent Rule*

To my knowledge, Texas is the only state to have enacted what is commonly called the Top 10 Percent Rule, so I'll explain to any non-natives what it means. Texas House Bill 588, passed in 1997, guarantees any Texas student who graduates in the top 10 percent of his or her high-school class automatic admission to any Texas state university. It is not a scholarship, and it is not a promise of graduation; it merely grants admission. Seats not filled by the Top 10 Percent Rule are (at UT anyway) still subject to affirmative action.

The only real issue with the Top 10 Percent Rule has been the law's unintentional side effect of excluding applicants to the state's larger flagship schools, such as UT or Texas A&M, who don't qualify for admission under Bill 588. That's because historically a majority of Texas's white high achievers have flocked to these schools, such that in 2008 alone, 81 percent of UT's freshman class came in under the Top 10 Percent Rule—leaving just 19 percent of the seats to be filled by other applicants. Since the law's enactment, many amendments to the Top 10 Percent Rule have been proposed but not adopted.

In 2007, then-president Powers wrote an op-ed piece that was published in the *Austin American-Statesman*. It suggested capping the number of students admitted to UT under the Top 10 Percent Rule at 75 percent of that year's total admissions. To do so would save at least a quarter of the seats for other applicants with equally impressive academic records, high SAT scores, extracurricular leadership, and the like who were being denied admission for no other reason than an artificially high level of competition induced by the passage of Bill 588. I then wrote an op-ed to the *Statesman* editor in support of Powers's opinion, stating that the Top 10 Percent Rule is a good idea in theory and that I didn't think we should do away with it but that it needed to be reformed.

With past president William Powers Jr. and current dean of the UT law school, Ward Farnworth

You probably saw the story on the news, but just in case you did not: Abigail Fisher is a young white woman who first applied for undergraduate admission to UT in 2008. Fisher did not graduate in the top 10 percent of her class, and so she had to compete for the percentage of seats left available in that year's incoming class. Despite an otherwise strong record of academic and extracurricular achievement, Fisher was denied fall admission. She then surmised that the decision had been made on the basis of her race. Affirmative action, she believed, had given "her" seat to a minority student, and so she and another white female applicant (who had also been denied) brought suit against the university.

When the Texas legislature met in 2009, a bill was introduced to officially cap admissions from the Top 10 Percent Rule at 75 percent. President Powers asked me to testify before the Higher Education Committee of the House and Senate on behalf of UT and in support of the bill. I presented each member of the committee with a copy of the op-ed that I'd written outlining why a cap on the Top 10 Percent Rule was imperative, as well as a copy of an article describing the 2003 case of *Grutter v. Bollinger*, which upheld the affirmative-action admissions policy of the University of Michigan Law School. I then shared my past experience as a black student at UT and explained why minorities were still applying to UT only in small numbers; UT's well-documented racist history, as well as many black students' desire to attend a school where they feel "comfortable" (generally speaking, an HBCU), meant that UT should not further alienate any willing minority applicants by abolishing affirmative action—not if they supported the diversification of Texas's top-flight schools.

More than a decade after the Top 10 Percent Rule's enactment, Texas legislators *did* pass a new law capping the bill at 75 percent. They told me afterward that my testimony was primarily responsible for persuading them. As for Abigail Fisher, she was offered the opportunity to reapply, this time with a 25 percent chance of acceptance. For whatever reason, she once again failed to make the cut, and she returned with new accusations about UT admitting a student with a lower GPA than hers. The local court granted a summary judgment that UT won. Fisher appealed all the way to the Supreme Court, but UT still won.

» *Judge Murphy Goes on Judge Judy*

It's important to me to live in a house and a community in which I feel comfortable and safe. In 2015, I believed my comfort and safety were endangered by my next-door neighbor, Chris Ferran. We went so far as to air our grievances on national television, and still nothing has been resolved. I include the story here, recognizing that it tells, as does most of this book, only one side of the story: mine.

It was several years ago that I first noticed my concrete driveway cracking and buckling. The only apparent explanation was the expansive growth of a tree located right at the line between the Ferran family's property and mine. It seemed the tree's roots were trying to come up under my driveway, and the buckling soon became so bad that I could no longer pull my car into the driveway. Last year, I asked Mr. Ferran to cut down the tree, remove the roots, and have my driveway repaired. As the tree was on his property, he was liable for the damages under Texas case law*—a reparation to which he at first agreed.

In an exchange of e-mails dated August 2015, Mr. Ferran confessed that he was out of work at the time and unable to afford any financial compensation. He offered to remove the tree and fix the driveway himself, and I accepted this offer. When months went by and no reparations were made, I again confronted Mr. Ferran, only to find out that he had no real intention of making good on his word. He did have the tree cut down, but the roots were not removed and my driveway had not been repaired. I continued to press the matter, until finally Mr. Ferran said we should have the dispute professionally arbi-

---

*C. Gulf & S. F. Ry. Co. v. Oakes, 52 L.R.A. 293 (1900). 94 Tex. 155, 58 S.W. 999, 86 Am. St. Rep. 835.

trated. His solution was to appear on the syndicated courtroom TV show *Judge Judy*.

The "Tree Root Ruckus," as Judge Judy later called it, was not Mr. Ferran's first offense. Our neighborhood association had previously censured him for repeated violations of the neighborhood code. I knew my case was solid, and I figured if Mr. Ferran wanted a televised audience, at least he'd be exposed for the troublemaker he was. We flew to LA in October for the taping, and our episode aired December 18, 2015. I sent a notice to everybody in the neighborhood so they could watch.

In the show, Mr. Ferran convinced Judge Judy that my driveway buckling could be due to weather and age (rather than root damage) by comparing my driveway to another neighbor's cracked driveway. That neighbor, by the way, had not given his permission and was surprised at being dragged into the situation. When Judge Judy questioned Mr. Ferran about prior neighborhood complaints levied against him, he brushed them off, saying, "Oh, it was just some loud noise, and I took care of it."

At that point, I should have called as a witness the contractor originally contacted by Mr. Ferran to assess the root damage. He would have testified as to the content of our discussions and made Mr. Ferran out to be the liar that he is when he said he could not know from where the damage came. Barring the contractor's testimony, however, Judge Judy ruled that I had failed to produce enough evidence to win the case, and Mr. Ferran was not legally required to do anything to help me out.

A few weeks later, a big septic truck visited the Ferran residence to repair the damages to Mr. Ferran's septic tank caused by the tree roots in question. I again noted that the tree was several feet from his septic tank but only one foot or so from my driveway. I then paid for my broken driveway to be torn up and, lo and behold, when the hunks of cement were pulled up, there were the exposed tree roots, clearly coming from his yard. I invited Mr. Ferran over to see the roots, assured that he could no longer deny his liability. I asked whether he was going to make any kind of contribution to the expense of removing the roots. His response? "I'll be away for three months and will talk with you when I return."

Although the issue remains unresolved, I cannot express my joy at proving that he was a liar. The Tree Root Ruckus is far from over.

PART IV » THERE ALL THE HONOR LIES

*Memories of our lives, of our works,
and our deeds will continue in others.*
—ROSA PARKS

This final section explores in more detail the awards bestowed upon me, the famous faces I met, and the politics I continued to fight for and against in each decade between 1975 and 2015.

Austin Black Lawyers Association: I may not have inherited my father's knack for the visual arts, but my creativity shines through most clearly when it comes to thinking up good ideas. Thirty-five years ago, I had the idea to organize an association of black lawyers in Austin. I also helped to organize another one for women lawyers in Travis County. Both continue to thrive and have made great strides in eliminating racial and gender bias in the legal profession.

Judicial forum during the early 1990s: Actually, the title of the program was "Bringing the Judges to the People." I was told about such a program by a judge from California while attending a national meeting of the Judicial Council of the National Bar. It was one of his programs that he established. It allows the public to learn more about what judges do. He wanted to challenge the fear that many have of the judicial system.

I thought that it would be a good program for the Austin community, especially for minorities, high-school students, and, of course, the general public. I presented the program to the Travis County Bar, now the Austin Bar, for approval and support. I received both. My friend, Judge Angelita Mendoza-Waterhouse, and I then became the chairs, and we asked Judge Mike Lynch to join us. For three consecutive years, we hosted a rotating panel of judges in Travis County at the University of Texas Thompson Center. We invited the public to attend and submit their handwritten questions about the judicial system. The newspapers advertised the forums to their general readership, but we also directly invited school groups, church groups, and representatives from associations like Mothers Against Drunk Driving. With topics such as Crime and Punishment, What Does a Sentence Really Mean?, and Getting to Know Your Judges, the idea was to improve relations between the public and the judges at that time.

The forums, whose names were coined by the newspaper, were so well received that we won an award from the State Bar of Texas. Later, the American Bar Associations' Judicial Committee paid for me to bring the program to their national meeting in Atlanta, Georgia, where I presented it to the Atlanta League of Women Voters so that they might implement the forums there too. Despite our success, Judge Mendoza-Waterhouse, Judge Lynch, and I ended the program in 1993 for a couple of reasons. First, it was simply too much work for three people to spend all that time contacting and organizing groups to attend. Second, even if we'd had all the time and energy in the world, the event had admittedly started to feel political. By including certain judges on our panels and not others, we felt as though we were unintentionally endorsing some candidates over others for elected office, so we let it go.

1992: Certificate of Commission, Yellow Rose of Texas. The Yellow Rose of Texas Commission is granted to a Texas woman nominated by a community member for outstanding volunteer service and recognized by the governor. I received the award in 1992, when Ann Richards was governor.

The award's name references Emily West Morgan, a young mulatto ("yellow") woman who played an important role in Texas winning its independence from Mexico in 1836.* Originally in the employ of American colonel James Morgan (of Morgan County, Texas), Emily caught the eye of Mexican general Santa Anna, who regularly invited her to his tent. In this way, Emily passed information from the Mexican camps to the Americans. She was entertaining Santa Anna in San Jacinto the morning that Colonel Morgan surprise attacked,

---

*A mulatto is a person with both Caucasian and African blood. The song was originally known as "The Yallow Rose of Texas," because light-skinned black women were called "yallow" by black men.

With Willie Nelson at the Conley Guerrero Senior Center

turning the war and ultimately claiming Texas, New Mexico, Arizona, Colorado, Utah, Nevada, and Wyoming for the United States. We never would have gotten away from Mexico if not for Emily!

I mention this story because Emily's contribution has never been publicly recognized in any celebration of Texas independence over the years. If her story was better known, our black children would be overjoyed with pride. Her legacy does live on in the Emily Morgan Hotel (located in San Antonio near the Alamo) and the song "The Yellow Rose of Texas." This song was written by an old black man who took his cue from "The Red Rose of Tennessee," sung by the Tennessee soldiers fighting alongside Texas in the war.

1990s: Country-folk singers Willie Nelson and Kris Kristofferson returned to their home state for a free concert at the Conley Guerrero

With President Bill Clinton

I had the honor of meeting civil rights activist Rev. Jesse Jackson, who ran for president in 1984 and 1988.

Senior Center. Other famous faces I met during this time include President Bill Clinton, the Reverend Jesse Jackson, and actor Samuel L. Jackson (his wife is a Spelman alum).

Spelman Legacy: Yes, I've done a lot of advocacy work for both UT and Huston-Tillotson over the years, but not for a second have I forgotten my Spelman College roots.

You'll remember that I was admitted to Spelman as a sixteen-year-old but that, because my age was listed incorrectly on my birth certificate, I missed my bragging rights (*smile*). My 87 percent (B+) average from the only black high school in Atlanta won me a four-year scholarship to Spelman that, due to my poor academic performance, soon ended. I did graduate, though, and I'm so proud of my Spelman degree. In gratitude for everything that diploma has made possible in my life, I have paid the college back many times over in terms of both money and service.

Since my graduation, I have contributed thousands of dollars to Spelman College. Most of the funds were earmarked for scholarships, including the Marguerite Simon Endowed Scholarship (which my class established in 1954 or 1959). On rare occasions, money went to the general fund. For a $1,000 donation that supported the renovation of Sisters Chapel, my name was inscribed on a great mosaic plaque of donors that currently hangs in the chapel's lobby. Now I am a member of the Guardian Society, composed of those alumnae who have promised to bequeath funds to Spelman in their wills.

As for service, I began working with the Atlanta Spelman alumnae chapter upon graduation. Mrs. Alberta Williams King, the mother of Martin Luther King Jr., hosted a couple of our meetings in her home. Alberta King was a great advocate for Spelman College, having herself graduated high school from Spelman Seminary and with a daughter (Christine King Farris) who still teaches at Spelman. After leaving Atlanta to teach at Southern University in Louisiana, I became a charter member of the Baton Rouge Spelman alumnae chapter. I then founded a third chapter in Houston upon moving to Prairie View. Later, I became a founder of the Austin/San Anto-

Judge Harriet Murphy, 2013 Spelman College honorary degree recipient

nio alumnae chapter. As a member of the executive committee of the Spelman National Alumnae Association from 2008 to 2012, I represented Spelman College at the inauguration of five new Texas university presidents—one at Southwestern University in Georgetown, one at Austin College, President Powers at UT, and two at Huston-Tillotson.

Spelman hasn't forgotten me, either. In 1993, I was inducted into the Spelman National Alumnae Hall of Fame. Oprah Winfrey was Spelman's commencement speaker that year, and Morgan Freeman was in attendance as the father of a Spelman graduate. I got to meet both of them! In 2013, former president Beverly Tatum nominated me for an honorary doctor of law degree from the college, which I received in May of that year. In addition, I had the honor of being reunion class speaker in 1969, and around 1989, I was the recipient of Spelman's Tiffany award.

1993: Thurgood Marshall passed. We named the annual luncheon of the National Judicial Council of the National Bar Association the Thurgood Marshall Luncheon. The last time I saw him, he told me, "You're just as pretty now as you were then!" I was feeling old, and his compliment made my day.

1994: National Women's Political Caucus and That Time I Ran for City Council. In 1983, the National Women's Political Caucus held their annual convention in San Antonio. The affair honored female officeholders nationwide and was called "Thanksgiving in July." One of the session moderators scheduled to address the conference attendees had to cancel at the last minute. Governor Ann Richards, who was acting as mistress of ceremonies that night, called me (a longtime active member of the Caucus) to ask if I would fill in. I immediately jumped in my car and drove down to San Antonio. Off-the-cuff, I spoke about how women bring a special sensitivity to the judiciary in particular, because we can apply our experiences with raising families to treating people like people and not case numbers. Governor Richards later complimented my speech; giving that speech remains one of the proudest moments of my life!

In 1994, a seat became available on the seven-member Austin City Council. Somehow, I let the mother of former Dallas mayor Ron Kirk talk me into running for that seat—an impudence for which I should be shot, given how it all shook out in the end. Beginning in the 1970s, Austin had implemented a "gentlemen's agreement" that provided for two minority seats on the council: one black, one Hispanic. As council member Charles Urdy was retiring that year, it was the black seat (known as Place 6) that had opened up. Eight other African Americans and I competed for that spot!

Less than one year after my own retirement from the bench, on

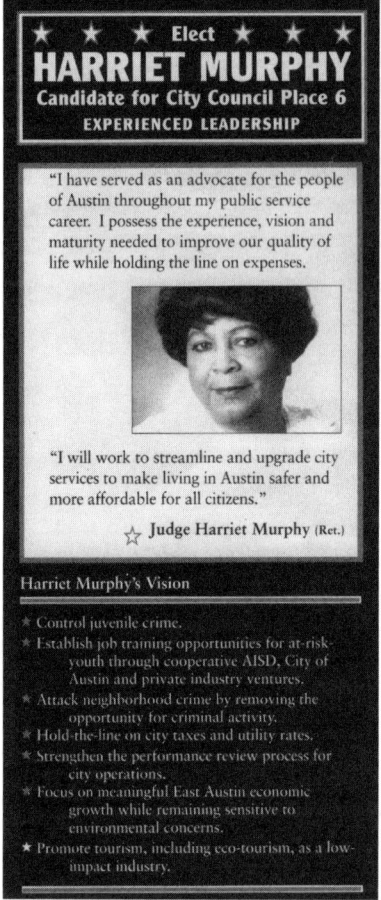

Campaign pamphlet

Wednesday, January 12, 1994, I announced my campaign. I said that I was running for city council because my experience as a judge had prepared me to help solve some of Austin's most pressing problems. I promised reduced crime rates, lower taxes, more reasonable utility rates, a focus on the environment, and job training for high-school dropouts. Reporter Joe Washington picked up my story, affirming that "Murphy has a long record of serving as an advocate for the disenfranchised in Austin through a variety of roles." That coverage was good, but it was the endorsement of the National Women's Political Caucus that I was counting on most heavily, as they had the power to sway up to 50 percent of the vote (that is, the female vote). The caucus had assured me that my decades-long devotion to their organization had earned me their official support. I even sent them $500 with which to print and distribute a newsletter stating just that. Not only did the National Women's Political Caucus *not* endorse me, but they publicly endorsed one of the male candidates instead. So much for white women championing well-qualified black women! And they never even returned my check!

When all was said and done, I took third place in the election with about 8,000 votes. The city held a run-off election between the top two candidates: Ron Davis and Eric Mitchell. I voted for Davis because he'd been my student at Huston-Tillotson. Mitchell, an insurance executive, won by securing the very powerful endorsement of the Austin Chamber of Commerce. He received contributions from all the local movers and shakers in Austin's traditional business community, and later, he received their votes.

Austin no longer holds citywide at-large elections. In November 2012, Austinites voted in favor of three propositions that reshaped the city's electoral process. Four new seats were created and ten districts established, with the understanding that each district would elect its own city-council representative and the mayor would fill the eleventh seat.

Mid-1990s: Jack and Jill of America Inc. and The Links Inc. The NAACP may be the most widely recognized civil rights organization in the country, but two more deserve some acclaim. First, Jack and Jill of America Inc. describes itself as "a membership organization of mothers with children ages 2–19, dedicated to nurturing future African American leaders by strengthening children through leadership development, volunteer service, philanthropic giving and civic duty."*

---

*http://jackandjillinc.org.

For Jack and Jill, I sponsored and coached black teenagers competing in persuasive speaking contests for college scholarships. I also co-chaired the Beautillion Ball in 1982; this ball was a fancy-dress event meant to showcase black high-school seniors and combat negative African American stereotypes in the media.

The Links Inc., founded in 1946, "is one of the oldest and largest volunteer service organizations of women who are committed to enriching, sustaining, and ensuring the culture and economic survival of African Americans and other persons of African ancestry."* I variously served as president and vice president of The Links from 1994–1997.

1995: In 1991, the Supreme Court appointed a gender bias task force "to investigate the existence of gender bias in the legal system and to recommend measures for its reduction and eventual elimination." Four years later, I was appointed to the Gender Bias Reform Implementation Committee.

1998: Habitat for Humanity. As a member of the Habitat for Humanity board and the Delta Sigma Theta Sorority Austin Alumnae chapter chair of the Housing Committee, I spearheaded a fundraiser to benefit Habitat for Humanity. The fundraiser netted $13,333 (more than one-third the price of the home), which we then combined with contributions from corporate sponsors Church's Chicken, Popeyes, and Pillsbury to build a home for the Middleton family in East Austin.

On February 21 of that year, the home was officially completed and dedicated. Delta sorority was involved every step of the way, from ground breaking to construction to providing refreshments on the day the Middletons moved in. For our efforts, we were recognized at the next national convention of the sorority.

Around the same time, as president of the Austin chapter of the Links, I also led a fundraiser with the Austin chapter of the Links

---

*http://www.linksinc.org.

The Austin Chapter of Delta Sigma Theta Sorority gather for the groundbreaking for a Habitat for Humanity Home to be built for Paula Middleton, a single mother of five. Left to right: Judge Harriet Murphy, Habitat for Humanity committee chair and Delta Austin alumnae; State Representative Dawnna Dukes; Paula Middleton, Habitat homeowner; Barbara Wooden, AFC Enterprises; Alonza Blankenship, general business director, Church's Chicken; Myrtle Williams Bell, Delta Austin alumnae; Joan Roberts Scott, Delta Austin alumnae and 1997–99 chapter president; and Kandace Tornquist, Austin Habitat for Humanity executive director. Photo used with permission from Delta Sigma Theta Sorority.

to benefit Habitat for Humanity. We organized a soiree at the Zach Scott Theatre that featured the music of Louis Jordan, a saxophonist perhaps best known for penning the musical short *Five Guys Named Moe*. His widow, Martha Jordan, of Las Vegas, attended the event as our honored guest, and we presented her with an award on behalf of Habitat and the Links.

2000: Black History Month and MLK Jr. In 2000, the African American Employee Program of the Department of Veterans Affairs recognized my year-after-year participation in Black History Month festivities (celebrated in February) as well as the annual remembrance of M. L. on Martin Luther King Jr. Day, always on the third Monday in January. I am the only person now living in Austin who can express the blessings of having known M. L. personally, and yet I have grown tired of speeches and appearances regarding that beautiful friendship. I have no letters from M. L., and I never wrote to him. I just saw him on many occasions, mostly at the airport as I was arriving in Atlanta and he was leaving or when I was leaving Atlanta as he was arriving.

It was on one of those flyby occasions at Hartsfield-Jackson that M. L., on learning of the recent death of my first husband, asked whether I might come to work for the Southern Christian Leadership Conference. He knew of my service with the Atlanta NAACP, particularly my women's auxiliary work. Even today there are moments I regret not joining the SCLC. Had I given up law school when M. L. asked me, I'd probably be as famous as Congressman John Lewis (the man who worked beside MLK Jr. for all those years before becoming a congressman—he's always called on now to help celebrate Martin Luther King Jr. Day), but at the time I was committed to getting a law degree. I believed that bringing change to east Texas would be my greatest contribution to The Struggle. Ironically, I never returned to Gregg County; I married Pat Murphy, and he refused to live in Longview.

2002: The Travis County Bar Association named me one of ten "legal legends" in the county and featured me in a documentary film produced by UT.

2000s: National Bar Association. The National Bar Association, on its fiftieth anniversary in 2001, granted me a Chairperson's Award for "distinguished service to the Judicial Council of the National Bar Association." At their seventy-eighth annual convention two years later, I was recognized with a Gertrude Rush Award for outstanding service to the association as a whole. In 2005, I won the Judge Raymond Pace Alexander Award for "outstanding contributions to judicial advocacy" and general humanitarianism.

The biggest honor of all, however, was my induction into the National Bar Association's Hall of Fame in 2010. To that special event

Induction into the National Bar Association Hall of Fame, 2010

in New Orleans, I was accompanied by my nephew Dr. Mark Berry, granddaughter Tahaja Murphy, best friends Dr. Carrie Johnson and Dr. Connie Romanski, and my surrogate daughter, Lateefah Neal Franks. After the event, Arleas Upton Kea and UT presented me with a beautiful commemorative photo book so I'd never forget just how honored I'd felt.

2004: Pioneer Award, UT Law School. UT established a Pioneer Award to recognize those alumni who "make a significant impact on the law school or community at large." At the State Bar of Texas Annual Meeting in 2004, I was the Pioneer honored for forty years of service to UT. In addition to all my work with the law school already mentioned in earlier chapters, I chaired a program to help attract and acclimate black students to UT. We invited student representatives from grades ten and up to tour the campus and learn why UT is a great place to study. Our work reflected especially well on President

Powers, who made a heroic effort during his tenure to reverse a century's worth of racial prejudice at UT. Powers was more loved and respected by blacks than any other UT president has been to date.

As a presidential associate, I also contribute financially to the university every year: to the UT School of Law, the Chancellor's Council, and the Board of Black Precursors, comprised of black UT alumni who graduated forty-plus years ago and who assist in planning black alumni events. Recently, the Precursors sponsored a successful weekend program celebrating the sixtieth anniversary of the first blacks to enter the freshman class in 1956.

Finally, I serve on the Black Alumni Network executive committee and the advisory committee of the Division of Diversity and Community Engagement. In addition to serving as a member of the Texas Exes council from July 2012 to June 2013, I am a lifetime member of the Texas Exes.

What I am most proud of is the fact that I was finally successful in getting the UT School of Law to recognize the first black student, Virgil Lott, to graduate from the law school. My desire to have the law school recognize Lott arose after I had read that the University of Alabama recognized the first black student to enter that school. The Virgil C. Lott program occurs every other year during the minority weekend at UT. A black graduate of the law school is honored with a medallion. Past recipients include former Texas Supreme Court Justice Wallace Jefferson, former state Senator Rodney Ellis, and Ron Kirk, first black mayor of Dallas.

2006: Pat and I buy the house that I still live in today. When we were looking for a house ten years ago, my only requirement was that the house be one story, since I had fallen down the stairs twice in our old home. We found one that I liked at Onion Creek, but Pat wouldn't go for it, so we ended up with the house I have now. It's too big for one person. If I had unlimited money, I'd give most of it to charity, saving just enough for a smaller, more beautiful home with a maid and chauffeur!

At the first Virgil C. Lott Award ceremony, 2009. With Dr. Gregory J. Vincent, vice president for diversity and community engagement; UT president Bill Powers; Michael Loftin; Texas Supreme Court Justice Wallace Jefferson, who won the first Virgil Lott Award; and UT law school dean Larry Sager.

2007: The YWCA calls me a "Phenomenal Woman" and awards me a lifetime achievement commendation.

2007–2008: The *Austin American-Statesman* twice includes me on its annual list of 500 important Austinites.

2007: The Black Pull in Politics. The *Austin American-Statesman* publishes an editorial I authored on historical trends regarding the black vote. Although today the labels "African American" and "Republican" would seem to fall at opposite ends of the spectrum, it wasn't always that way. Following Republican president Abraham Lincoln's emancipation of American slaves, most early black voters identified as Republican. Senator Thad Cochran capitalized on that historical allegiance to capture the black vote in Mississippi, thereby securing his reelection despite otherwise stacked odds.

For more on the shift among African Americans from majority Republican to majority Democrat, you can reference the original article included here. The point I want to make is that had David Dewhurst, lieutenant governor of Texas from 2003 to 2015, appealed to black voters in his 2012 Senate campaign against Ted Cruz, even as a Republican he would have stood a better chance. He made no effort at all to reach out to the native black community, however, which could have made all the difference.

I know this to be true thanks to one positive and one ultimately negative experience I had the two times that I, a staunch liberal, was persuaded to vote conservative. The first time was in the 1962 runoff for Gregg County judge between Democrat Peppy Blount and his Republican rival. Blount was a known racist and outspoken fundamentalist, believing that if something was a sin in the Bible, it should be conflated with a punishable violation of the law as well. Several black community members and I decided to set up a campground to use as a headquarters for garnering the Republican vote—simply because we did not want Peppy in office.

The second (and unfortunate) instance, of which I am today ashamed, involved my championing one of the most conservative associate justices of the Supreme Court that this country has ever seen: Clarence Thomas. Only the second African American justice (after Thurgood Marshall) to serve on the Supreme Court, Thomas was many years ago being considered for approval for the Supreme Court. He was up against Judge Edith Jones of the US Fifth Circuit in New Orleans, a white woman known for speaking openly about black Americans' blanket tendency to criminality. President Davis of the National Bar Association appointed me to the judicial selection committee to argue against the recommendation of Jones by the Bar, which we did. The legal defense representation knew Clarence Thomas's background better than we did, however. She knew that despite being black, Thomas had never had the interests of black America at heart, and she literally shed tears, so opposed was she to his nomination. We should have listened to her, because in the end Thomas has never voted for the rights of black people—altogether

At the 2014 University of Texas Evening of Honors with the Precursors. From left to right: UT student Jordan Metoyer, William Spearman, Lonnie Fogle, Maudie Ates Fogle, Fred Alexander, Judith Jenkins, Harriet Murphy, Dr. Gregory J. Vincent, Peggy Holland, and Leon Holland.

the opposite of Thurgood, who was concerned with the promotion of freedom for all people. So even though my second trip to the White House was to attend Thomas's investiture, all these years I've kept my initial support for him a secret, as it is partly my fault that we have him on the bench today.

2011: The City of Austin Economic Growth and Redevelopment Services Office, through the Art in Public Places program, commissions a 6′ × 25′ glass-and-ceramic-tile mosaic to celebrate the opening of the African American Cultural and Heritage Facility. My portrait makes it into the mosaic, which is on 11th Street.

2013: With three other women, I am inducted into the Austin Women's Hall of Fame.

2014: I establish a music scholarship fund at Huston-Tillotson in the name of Pat and Harriet Murphy. Pat was a music major at H-T, and I know he would be proud. The fund grants $500 a year to each of two

Pat and I have always been proud supporters of Huston-Tillotson University.

students: one in the choir and one from the music department. Anyone who wants to donate to the fund is encouraged to do so through the Huston-Tillotson University Development Office, 900 Chicon Street, Austin, Texas, 78702, or at http://htu.edu/offices/ia.

2015: When President Gregory Fenves came aboard at UT, he invited me to the football suite and we established a good relationship. I had previously met him when he was provost under President Powers in 2013–2014. I was very elated when I learned he would become president of the university. I told him about my op-ed and he sent me a note. We have continued our discussions throughout the years; recently, we talked about my participation in the law school's minority weekend, which led to another note he sent to me in 2017.

2015: Founding Fathers Award, NAACP. On December 5, 2015— smack-dab in the middle of writing this book, actually—I receive the Founding Fathers Award from the NAACP. I had years ago received the Arthur B. DeWitty Award. The Founding Fathers Award

With current UT president Gregory L. Fenves

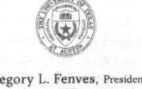

Gregory L. Fenves, President
The University of Texas at Austin

Dec. 22, 2015

Dear Judge Murphy,

It was good to see you at the Community Leadership Awards last week, and thank you for your 2007 article about top-10. It is as true today as it was when you wrote the article. I hope we can all work towards an admission process that results in excellent and diverse student body at UT. Merry Christmas,

Greg

Note from President Fenves

is named for two celebrated civil rights spokesmen from Austin. It recognized my lifelong contributions to the cause, and I accepted it before a roomful of supporters at the Austin Convention Center. In my acceptance speech, I reminisced about the long-ago fireside chat I'd attended at Spelman College with its white female president, just before my senior graduation. During that fireside chat, she admonished us that we'd soon be going out into the world and must never forget to give back to the community. Many people had sacrificed for us to be able to graduate, she said, and we were duty-bound to pay the debt back. I trace my entire life's efforts toward community service to that single moment at Spelman.

Afterword

Pat, my husband, died nearly five years ago. Pneumonia finally claimed him after a battle lasting more than two years. When Pat was sick, he could eat only soft foods, and then only through a tube. I've been on my own ever since.

When I think about what I hope to be remembered for, it's that (with the exception of my first husband) I've never had to be dependent on anyone else, and I've always been authentically myself. Whatever dreams I had for myself as a child, I made them come true through hard work and perseverance. I've taken care of myself emotionally, financially, and otherwise, and I've taken advantage of every opportunity to give back to the community of which I'm so proud to be a part. Because of that involvement, I've never forgotten where I came from either. One day I was out shopping with a friend at a department store, and after wrapping up a conversation with the saleslady, my friend said, "You know what, Harriet? You didn't act like a judge with that woman." *Why should I?* I thought. *I don't have to put on airs or pretend to be something I'm not. I'm Harriet M. Murphy!*

Although my community involvement has waned in recent years, I still fill in as a judge at the Precinct 1 court whenever they call. That's why the sheriff's office has kept me on their list of active judges; they help watch over us, especially in the wake of Julie Kocurek's shooting. A state district judge, Kocurek was standing in her driveway one evening in November 2015 when a drive-by shooter fired four bullets at her. The suggested motive was retaliation following her delivery of a guilty verdict in a recent court case. Deputies made daily rounds of all the judges right after the shooting. They come around less frequently now that it seems it wasn't a mass terrorism deal but just a one-off shooting. Then again, I've never been a judge on a high-enough level to send somebody to prison or sentence them to death, so luckily, I was never personally afraid for my life.

When not serving as a substitute judge, I worship with the Ebenezer Baptist Church in Austin, where I formerly served as chair of the legal ministry, and on some occasions, I teach Sunday school. Under the former minister, I was the pro bono lawyer for Ebenezer Baptist, advising any parishioner who had to go to court.

I also love to attend competitive bridge parties. Pat and I actually organized a couple's bridge club one year; it's still going, although most of the husbands are dead now. I like to joke about the "problem" of my busy social life interfering with my social advocacy work, but really it's time to pass the reins to someone else. Time has shown no discrimination; these bones age and ache like the next person's. Looking back on my life, I feel proud to have acted well my part (although I wonder now how I did it all!). There all the honor lies.

Appendix I » Reverend Walter M. Mitchell Sr.: Minister and Civil Rights Activist

Because my maternal grandfather's efforts inspired my early activism, I wanted to include a testament to the great man he was. Reverend Walter Mitchell Sr. has been written about in a number of publications, including Oxford University Press's *African American National Biography*; the *Atlanta Journal-Constitution*; a 1952 publication, *Go Down Moses: A Study of 21 Successful Negro Rural Pastors*; and a 1988 book called *The Prevailing South*.

Here is his story.

Walter Melvin Mitchell (1893–1983) was a minister, carpenter, and civil rights activist. He was born in Greene County, Georgia, and was greatly influenced by his grandfather, Pano Mitchell, who revered his African heritage. At the age of thirteen, Walter became the chief farmer for his family. At age sixteen, he moved in with an uncle who was a skilled carpenter and brick mason; during that time, Walter learned carpentry and masonry skills.

In 1918 he returned to Greene County, where he began sharecropping. He attended extension classes at Morehouse College one night a week to become a minister. Forty-seven people began the classes, but Walter was one of only seven who completed the four-year track. He was ordained in 1922.*

Wanting to improve his ministry, he began attending a rural pastor's institute at Fort Valley College, Georgia, which led to a new philosophy as a rural pastor. Mitchell recalled to Ralph Felton, "After I came home, I began reading the farm papers. I got acquainted with the Soil Conservation Agent, the Farmers Home Administrator, the Jeannes Supervisor [*sic*]† and everybody else in the county

---

*Felton, p. 66.

†Jeanes supervisors were African American teachers hired as supervisors in African American schools to improve black communities. A Quaker philanthropist

My grandfather, the Reverend Walter Mitchell Sr., Easter 1961

who could help my people. My members began to call me 'a farmer preacher.'"*

Mitchell encouraged members of his three churches in Smyrna, Carters Hill, and Rocky Branch to give up sharecropping and buy their own farms—and even loaned money to men to buy farms. Sev-

---

named Anna T. Jeanes provided the funding for the program in 1907. By 1952 there were 510 Jeanes teachers in the South, many of whom became leaders in the civil rights movement. The program ended in 1968.

*Felton, p. 66.

eral became extremely successful. Felton wrote, "It is reported that he has effected some changes in the farm practices of fifty families to whom he preaches on Sunday mornings." Mitchell also put his carpentry skills to use to benefit the families who were members of his church. Felton wrote, "Their pastor, like the carpenter of Nazareth, is helping to lighten their burden."*

In 1937, Walter married his third wife, Hazeltine, and moved to

---

*Felton, p. 69.

My grandfather, his third wife, and their daughter, Rosalyn. Photo courtesy of Rosalyn Mitchell.

With my grandfather

Morgan County thereafter. After World War II, he became more focused on civil rights and the "separate but equal" laws of the state of Georgia.* He served as chairman of the Civic League of Morgan County, which prepared blacks to vote. Remember that this was in the Jim Crow South. Felton wrote, "Out of 3,000 eligible Negro voters, 800 are now registered for voting. In the last election, 200 voted, the other 600 were afraid to go to the polls."†

The Civic League worked for and received equal pay for African American teachers and procured bus transportation for students in rural areas to attend the only high school available to African American students in the county. Walter began pushing for better school facilities too. He began receiving threats on his life, and the daughter of Walter and Hazeltine, Rosalyn, recalls that he taught her and

---

*Patterson, http://www.oxfordaasc.com/article/opr/t0001/e3376.
†Felton, p. 68.

her mother how to handle a shotgun. Walter was involved in a high-speed chase incident between Monroe and Madison one night. After that he decided to move his family to Atlanta for safety.*

In the 1970s, Walter was honored by the Madison chapter of the NAACP for his tireless efforts fighting for black education. Raymond Andrews wrote in a piece that appeared in the *Atlanta Journal-Constitution* and in a book titled *The Prevailing South* that "the local ceremony was attended by the town's leading whites, including the mayor and members of the integrated county school board. Reverend Mitchell has since died, but his memory lives on in his hometown of Madison."†

---

*Andrews, p. 175.
†Andrews, p. 177.

Appendix II » List of Awards

Certificate of Public Service, appointed a member of the advisory council of the Bureau of African Affairs, Department of State, United States, October 15, 1970.

Certificate of Appointment, Energy Study Commission, City Council, City of Austin, December 21, 1972.

Certificate of Appreciation, special efforts on behalf of good government, State of Texas, January 18, 1973.

Certificate of Recognition, contributions to the celebration of the American bicentennial in Austin, Austin Bicentennial Commission, September 17, 1976.

Elected Presidential Elector, State of Texas, November 2, 1976.

Outstanding Contributions to the Austin Community, Delta Beta Chapter, Phi Delta Kappa Inc., February 19, 1982.

Certificate of Appreciation, valuable and distinguished service, City Council, City of Austin, February 28, 1983.

Mentor, SASE (Spelman Alumna Student Externship Program), 1983.

Honorary Citizen of New Orleans, City of New Orleans, July 30, 1984.

Certificate of Appreciation, founding sponsor, Austin Area Urban League Inc., February 17, 1985.

Presentation of the Texas Flag Flown above the Texas State Capitol, convening of the sixty-ninth legislature, Rep. Ron D. Givens, State of Texas House of Representatives, May 1, 1985.

Certificate of Citation, Friendship and Unending Inspiration, Rep. Ron D. Givens, State of Texas House of Representatives, 1985.

Honorary Citizen of Chicago, City of Chicago, July 26, 1985.

Charter Member, Board Member, Friend, and Supporter, Austin Area Urban League, October 30, 1985.

Outstanding Alumni Award, Thurgood Marshall Legal Society, University of Texas School of Law, April 11, 1986.

Honorary Citizen of Atlanta, City of Atlanta, May 18, 1986.

Outstanding Service, Austin alumnae, Delta Sigma Theta Inc., 1983–1987.

Chairman's Award, distinguished service to the community, Greater Austin Council on Alcoholism and Drug Abuse Inc., February 24, 1990.

Outstanding Women of Color Recognition Award from the Austin Women's Addiction Referral and Education Center, October 25, 1991.

Presiding Judge, dedicated service to the court and City of Austin, Austin Municipal Court, March 12, 1992.

Certificate of Commission, Yellow Rose of Texas, State of Texas, December 4, 1992.

Induction, Spelman National Alumni Hall of Fame, 1993.

Certificate of Life Membership, National Association for the Advancement of Colored People, October 1993.

Bluebonnet Award for Achievement, WOMEN WHO DID: A Celebration of Achievement, Leadership Educational Arts Program (LEAP), March 11, 1995.

Certificate of Recognition, outstanding public servant, Black Heritage 1996 celebration, Texas General Land Office, February 27, 1996.

Outstanding Leadership as President, the Austin chapter of The Links Inc., 1994–1997.

Certificate of Appreciation, participation in the third annual Austin State Hospital Black Awareness Program, Texas Department of Mental Health and Mental Retardation, February 27, 1997.

Chair, Delta Sigma Theta Sorority Inc., Habitat for Humanity Committee, February 21, 1998.

Board of Directors, Austin Habitat for Humanity, 1996–2000.

Certificate of Appreciation, participation in Black History Month, African American Employment Program, Department of Veterans Affairs, February 23, 2000.

Inclusion, International Who's Who of Public Service, 2000.

Chairperson's Award, distinguished service to the Judicial Council of the National Bar Association, fiftieth anniversary, August 1, 2001.

Certificate of Appreciation, participation in the sixty-fifth annual NAACP Convention, Texas State NAACP, October 4–6, 2001.

Advisory Board, Believe in Me Project Inc., 2002.

Presidential Award, outstanding service to the Association, National Bar Association, Seventy-Eighth Annual Convention, August 4, 2003.

Pioneer Award, the first to make a significant impact on the law school or community at large, University of Texas School of Law, State Bar of Texas Annual Meeting, June 24, 2004.

Certificate of Commendation, Leadership, Dedication, and Exemplary Service to Family, Community, and the Legal Profession, State Bar of Texas Board of Directors, April 8, 2005.

Judge Raymond Pace Alexander Award, outstanding contributions to judicial advocacy, Judicial Council of the National Bar Association, August 3, 2005.

Induction, National Bar Association Hall of Fame, 2010.

Honorary Degree Recipient, Spelman College, 2013.

Induction, Austin Women's Commission Hall of Fame, October 23, 2013.

Appendix II » 141

Distinguished Citizen Award, Kappa Alpha Psi Fraternity Inc., Seventy-Eighth Southwestern Province Council, Austin, Texas, March 26–30, 2014.

Precursors Award, The University of Texas at Austin Division of Diversity and Community Engagement, 2014.

Founding Fathers Award, NAACP, December 5, 2015.

Honoree, first African American female judge in Texas, St. John Baptist District Association, twenty-sixth annual Spring Banquet, April 8, 2016.

Undated

"Gift and Giver of Knowledge" Award, graduating class of 1966.

Honorary Lifetime Member, Blackhorse Brigade, Headquarters Air Cab Combat Brigade.

References

"10 TCBA Legends Honored, Depicted in UT Film." *The Villager* 30, no. 4 (June 14, 2002): 1.

Andrews, Raymond. "Black Boy and Man in the Small Town South," in *The Prevailing South: Life and Politics in a Changing Culture*, edited by Dudley Clendinen. Atlanta: Longstreet Press, 1988.

Andrews, Raymond. "The Prevailing South." *The Atlanta Journal-Constitution*, July 18, 1988.

"Austin Women's Hall of Fame Selects Four for Induction." *NOKOA Observer* 26, no. 33 (October 16, 2013): 1.

Banks, Dorothy Charles. "Murphy Receives Presiding Judge Appointment." *The Villager* 16, no. 7 (June 17, 1988): 1.

"Black Intellectuals Slam Bantustans." *Cape Times*, n.d.

Breaux, Brenda J. "Cooke Forms 12-Member Task Force on Homeless." *Austin American-Statesman*, March 15, 1989.

Camp, Lynn Robinson. *Morgan County, Georgia*. Black America Series. Chicago: Arcadia Publishing, 2014.

Eaton, Collin. "Former Austin Judge Talks Texas Admissions." *The Daily Texan*, August 2, 2010.

"Ex-Judge Helps Out Pearce." *Austin American-Statesman*, n.d.

Felton, Ralph A. *Go Down Moses: A Study of 21 Successful Negro Rural Pastors*. Madison, NJ: Drew Theological Seminary, 1952.

Hanna, Mark. "Judge Murphy Rises above Prejudice." *Austin American-Statesman*, February 11, 1983.

"Joint Resolution Celebrating the Founding of the Austin Area Urban League." *The Villager*, June 3, 2011.

"Judge Harriet Murphy, Member of a Recent Air Force Civic Leaders Tour Conducted by the Air Force, Finds Herself with One More Role to Play." *Networker* 9, no. 2 (March 1987): 8.

"Judge Harriet Murphy: A Pioneer of Distinction." *Ujima Magazine*, September 2009.

"Judge Murphy Receives Raymond P. Alexander Award." *The Villager*, October 7, 2005.

"Local Judge Receives Award." *The Villager*, June 4, 1993.

Marshall, Thurgood. Letter to Harriet Mitchell Moore. March 10, 1967.
Mitchell, Harriet. "The Development of Nationalism in French Morocco." *Phylon: The Clark Atlanta University Review of Race and Culture* 16, no. 4 (1955): 427–34.
Murphy, Harriet. "Cochran's Win Evokes History of Black Fealty to Republicans." *Austin American-Statesman*, June 30, 2007.
Murphy, Harriet. "Eliminate the Top 10% Rule in University Admissions." *Austin American-Statesman*, July 4, 2014.
Murphy, Harriet. "Painful Reminder: Skin Color Matters." *Austin American-Statesman*, July 29, 2015.
"Murphy Inducted into Spelman's Hall of Fame." n.d.
Obregon, Enedelia J. "Remembering Dr. King." *Austin American-Statesman*, April 4, 1988.
Patterson, Rosalyn Mitchell. "Walter M. Mitchell." In *African American National Biography*, edited by Henry Louis Gates Jr. and Evelyn Brooks Higginbotham. Cambridge, MA: Hutchins Center for African & African American Research, Harvard University, 2005.
Pego, David. "Dos Culturas: One Pedagogy." *Black Issues in Higher Education* 13, no. 25 (February 8, 1996): 10–11.
Perkins, Laura. "Spelman Alumnae Back 'Cosby' Spinoff." *Austin American-Statesman*, October 1, 1987.
"Texas Doctor Dies after Checkup Shows Leukemia." *JET* 26, no. 13 (August 13, 1964): 25.
The Texas Politics Project. *Texas Politics*. University of Texas at Austin College of Liberal Arts. 2nd ed. 2015. http://texaspolitics.utexas.edu/textbook.
"Trial Watchers." *Austin American-Statesman*, January 31, 1995.
Ibid., February 15, 1995.
Ibid., March 7, 1995.
Ibid., May 2, 1995.
Ibid., June 20, 1995.
Ibid., July 15, 1995.
"University of Texas at Austin Continues to Honor Legacy of Firsts." *The Villager* 41, no. 52 (May 16, 2014): 1.
White, Jerry. "Municipal Judges' Dockets Lacking in Drama." *Austin American-Statesman*, n.d.
"YWCA of Greater Austin Honors 10 Outstanding 'Phenomenal Women.'" *The Villager* 35, no. 27 (November 23, 2007): 1.